Shortcuts to S

Science
for Junior Certificate

Eamonn Healy

GILL & MACMILLAN

To Bernie, Paul, Aisling, Grace and Roseanne

Gill & Macmillan Ltd
Hume Avenue
Park West
Dublin 12
with associated companies throughout the world
www.gillmacmillan.ie

© Eamonn Healy 2007
Artwork by Replika Press Pvt Ltd, India
978 0 7171 4171 5

Typeset in Replika Press Pvt Ltd, India

The paper used in this book is made from the wood pulp of managed forests. For every tree felled, at least one tree is planted, thereby renewing natural resources.

Contents

Biology

Introduction

Structure of the Exam

What is the breakdown of the marks in the Junior Certificate Examination in Science?

1. **Coursework A**: 10 per cent (60 marks out of 600). This consists of thirty mandatory experiments which must be carried out by the students and written up in a notebook for inspection purposes.

   All the mandatory experiments are included in this book, along with other experiments which may be examined. When writing a report on an experiment, include the following:

   - Date.
   - Names of person or people doing the experiment.
   - Aim of experiment.
   - Method.
   - Result.
   - Conclusion.

2. **Coursework B**: 25 per cent (150 marks out of 600). This can consist of:
   - Two investigations selected from three separate investigations in biology, chemistry and physics specified by the State Exam Commission; or
   - A single investigation of the student's own choosing which must meet guidelines laid down by the State Exam Commission.

   The student will be required to submit a report of this work in a pro forma booklet supplied by the State Exam Commission. This report will be included with and corrected along with the written examination paper.

3. **The written examination paper**: 65 per cent (390 marks out of 600). The examination paper will consist of three sections – Biology, Chemistry and Physics. The marks are divided equally between the three sections (130 marks each). The total time given to the exam is two hours.

   The following table gives a breakdown of marks in each section and suggested time allowances for each:

Section	Total marks	Number of questions	Marks		Time (minutes)	
Biology	130	3	Q1	52	Q1	15
			Q2	39	Q2	10
			Q3	39	Q3	10
Chemistry	130	3	Q4	52	Q4	15
			Q5	39	Q5	10
			Q6	39	Q6	10
Physics	130	3	Q7	52	Q7	15
			Q8	39	Q8	10
			Q9	39	Q9	10

Preparation for the Exam

It is important to note that there is no choice on the paper and therefore it is
essential that the *whole* course be studied. This book provides a concise study of
the whole course as per the syllabus. It is essential to start your revision in good
time to give yourself an opportunity to cover all sections thoroughly.

The first question in each section has questions which test your knowledge of
definitions and other data, such as functions of body parts, etc. Therefore, it is
essential that you revise all the short definitions on the course. These definitions
and other essential data are put together in a separate section in the book for easy
reference. Learn the definitions exactly, as precise answers are required in the
exam.

Make use of sample papers and past papers. A sample paper with answers is
provided with this text to provide detail on how questions should be answered
and how the marks are allotted.

Exam Tips to Maximise Your Scoring Potential

Many candidates do not do themselves justice in an exam through bad exam
technique. The following will help you improve your exam performance.

1. Allow about five minutes at the start of the exam to read the questions carefully. Decide which questions you can do best and start with these questions to give yourself a good start. Underline all the key words in the question to ensure you are answering what is asked.

2. Don't spend too much time on any questions. Stick to the time guide given in the table on p. vi. If you are struggling with a question, leave it and return to it later.

3. Allow ten minutes at the end of the exam to read all your answers again and recheck all your calculations. Try to attempt all parts. Write something down – it may merit marks.

4. Scientific terms must be defined fully and exactly. Note that the marks are usually assigned in units of three.

   Example: Define catalyst (6 marks).

   Answer: A catalyst speeds up a chemical reaction (3) without being used up itself (3).

5. A correct formula is usually accepted instead of a written definition.

   Example: Define density.

   Answer: density = mass ÷ volume
   This answer merits the same marks as 'mass per unit volume'.

6. When doing calculations, it is important to:
   - Give the formula.
   - Give the various stages in the calculation.
   - State the answer clearly and give the units, as the units carry marks.

   If you only give the answer and it is wrong, you will lose all the marks, whereas you will get marks for the formula and the stages if you present the answer as described.

   Example: Find the weight of a stone of mass 180 kg given that the acceleration due to gravity = 10 ms^{-2}. (6 marks)

   Answer: weight = mass × acceleration due to gravity
   $$= 180 \times 10 \text{ (3 marks)}$$
   $$= 1800 \text{ N (3 marks for unit)}$$

7. Draw large, clear, labelled diagrams. You don't have to be an artist, but the examiner must be able to recognise the apparatus and your labels must point clearly to what is being named. Don't waste time colouring diagrams.

8. It is important to practise drawing graphs as part of your exam preparation. When drawing a graph:
   - Use graph paper and pencil.
   - Draw the axes as requested in the question and label them clearly.
   - Make the graph as large as possible by planning the scale beforehand. Mark in the scale clearly.
   - Plot the points clearly and join them.

   Example: The following table gives values of the velocity of a body at certain times:

Velocity	1	2	4	5	6
Time	4	8	16	20	24

   Draw a graph of velocity against time (horizontal axis). (12 marks)

   Marking of question:
   - Axes correct – labels or numbers. ($2 \times 3 = 6$ marks)
   - Points plotted correctly. (3 marks)
   - Line drawn through points. (3 marks)

9. Formulas for compounds and elements are usually accepted instead of names.

10. In each section on the exam, experiments on biology, chemistry and physics will be examined, particularly the mandatory experiments, which are all included in this text. When describing a particular experiment, it is important that you include:
    - A step-by-step written description of the method.
    - A clearly labelled diagram of the apparatus used.
    - Result and conclusion.

    Example: Describe an experiment to test for conductors and insulators of electricity. (9 marks)

    Answer:
    1. Set up the circuit as shown with battery and bulb. (3 marks)
    2. Place a conductor, e.g. copper, in the gap between A and B.
    3. Result: The bulb lights, proving copper is a conductor. (3 marks)

4. Place an insulator, e.g. plastic, between A and B.

   Result: This time the bulb does not light, proving plastic is an insulator. (3 marks)

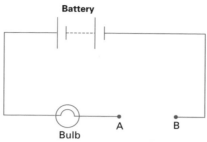

Place the test material between A and B

Please note that Higher Level material is indicated with a line beside the text, as shown:

Hooke's Law for a Spiral Spring

Hooke's law: The extension in a spiral spring is directly proportional to the force, provided the elastic limit of the spring is not exceeded.

Problem on Hooke's law: If a force of 5 N produces an extension of 15 cm, what extension would a 16 N force cause?

PHYSICS

Chapter 1
Mass, Volume and Density

Physics is the science of exact measurement of such quantities as length, mass and time. The SI (Systeme Internationale) system of units is used.

Quantity	SI unit	Symbol
Length	Metre	m
Mass	Kilogram	kg
Time	Second	s
Area	Square metre	m^2
Volume	Cubic metre	m^3

Measurement of Length

Length is measured in metres (m), where 1 metre = 100 centimetres (cm). A straight line can be measured using a metre stick or ruler, but for a curved line, an opisometer must be used.

Experiment: Measure the length of a curved line.

1. Ensure that the opisometer wheel is at the zero position.
2. Wheel the opisometer from one end of the line to the other.

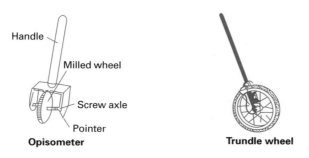

Handle
Milled wheel
Screw axle
Pointer
Opisometer

Trundle wheel

3. Wheel the opisometer back to the zero position along a metre stick.
4. Read off the measurement.

Engineers use a bigger version of an opisometer, called a trundle wheel, for longer line measurements on roads.

A Vernier callipers is used to measure the diameter of a sphere or pipe, as shown in the diagram.

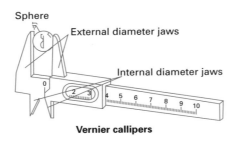

Vernier callipers

Mass and its Measurement

Mass is the amount of matter in a body. Mass is measured in kilograms (kg), where 1 kg = 1000 g. Mass of a body is measured using a balance or weighing scales.

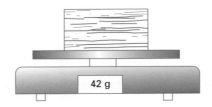

Measurement of Volume

Volume is the amount of space taken up by a body. Volume is measured in cubic metres (m^3) or cubic centimetres (cm^3).

To measure the volume of a regular body like a rectangular box, the length, breadth and height are measured with a ruler or metre stick and then the volume is calculated by the following formula:

volume = length × breadth × height

volume of box = $10 \times 15 \times 20 = 3000$ cm^3

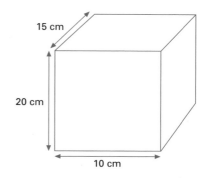

15 cm

20 cm

10 cm

Experiment: Measure the volume of an irregular body, e.g. a stone or potato.

1. Set up the apparatus as shown.
2. Immerse stone slowly in overflow can.
3. Collect displaced water in graduated cylinder.
4. Read off the volume. This is the volume of a stone.

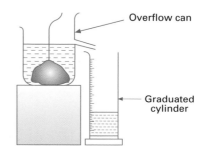

Overflow can

Graduated cylinder

Density and Flotation

Density of a body is the mass per unit volume, measured in g/cm^3.

$$\text{density} = \frac{\text{mass}}{\text{volume}}$$

Problem: Find the density of a body of mass 20 g and volume 4 cm^3.

$$\text{density} = \frac{\text{mass}}{\text{volume}} = \frac{20 \text{ g}}{4 \text{ cm}^3} = 5 \text{ g/cm}^3$$

Mandatory experiment: Find the density of a variety of solids and liquids.

(A) Find the density of a regular block, e.g. metal block.

1. Measure the mass of the block on a balance. Mass = 60 g.
2. Measure the length, breadth and height of the block with a ruler.

volume = L × B × H

$\qquad$ = 2 × 2 × 5

$\qquad$ = 20 cm^3

Therefore: density = $\dfrac{\text{mass}}{\text{volume}}$ = $\dfrac{60}{20}$ = 3 g/cm^3

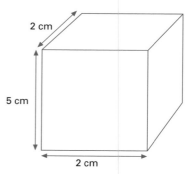

2 cm

5 cm

2 cm

(B) Find the density of an irregular body, e.g. a stone.

1. Find the mass of the stone using a balance.
2. Then find the volume of the stone by gently placing the stone in an overflow can, as shown in the diagram. Read the volume on the graduated cylinder.
3. Find the density of the stone by dividing the mass by the volume.

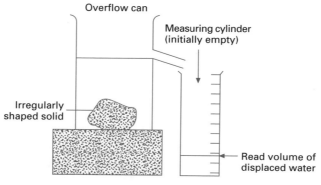

Overflow can

Measuring cylinder (initially empty)

Irregularly shaped solid

Read volume of displaced water

(C) Find the density of a liquid, e.g. water.

1. Find the mass of a clean dry beaker using a balance.
2. Add 20 cm^3 of water into the beaker using a burette, as shown in the diagram. A pipette can also be used to measure volume.
3. Find the mass of the beaker and the water.
4. Subtract the mass of the beaker from the mass of the beaker plus water to get the mass of the water.
   Mass = 20 g. Divide the mass by the volume to get the density. The density of water = $\dfrac{20}{20}$ = 1 g/cm^3.

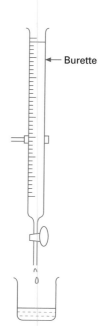

Burette

Floating or Sinking Bodies

An object will float in a liquid or gas if it is less dense than the liquid or gas. An object that is denser than the liquid or gas will sink in the liquid or gas.

Example: Copper (density = 8.9 g/cm^3) is denser than water (1 g/cm^3), so it sinks. Cork (density = 0.2 g/cm^3) is less dense than water, so it floats.

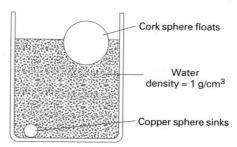

Cork sphere floats

Water
density = 1 g/cm^3

Copper sphere sinks

Mercury is a liquid with a much higher density than water. Its density is 13.6 g/cm^3. Therefore, a copper coin would float on mercury but would sink in water. Helium is a gas used in balloons, as it is less dense than air and therefore the balloon floats in air.

Oil (0.8 g/cm^3) is less dense than water and therefore floats on the surface of water.

Chapter 2
Velocity and Acceleration

Speed is the distance travelled in a certain time.

Velocity is the speed in a certain direction.

Example: Find the velocity of a body which travels 40 m due north in 20 seconds.

velocity $= \frac{40}{20} = 2$ m/s

Acceleration is the change in velocity per second.

$$\text{acceleration} = \frac{\text{change in velocity}}{\text{time}}$$

Acceleration is measured in m/s/s, m/s^2 or ms^{-2}.

Example: Find the acceleration of a body that changes its velocity from 20 m/s to 50 m/s in 5 seconds.

$$\text{acceleration} = \frac{\text{change in velocity}}{\text{time}}$$

$$= \frac{50 - 20}{5} = 6 \text{ m/s}^2$$

Distance/Time Graphs

The following table gives the distance travelled by a cyclist at different times:

Time (s)	0	1	2	3	4	5
Distance (m)	0	5	10	15	20	25

Graph the results on graph paper, putting time on the horizontal. Use the graph to find the distance travelled in 3.5 seconds.

Distance travelled in 3.5 seconds = 17.5 m (see graph).

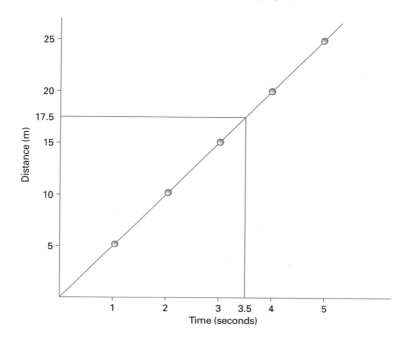

Velocity/Time Graphs

The following table gives values of the velocity of a body at certain times:

Velocity	1	2	3	4	5	6
Time	4	8	12	16	20	24

Question:

(a) Draw a graph of velocity against time (horizontal axis).

(b) Use the graph to find the velocity at 4.5 seconds.

(c) Use the graph to find the acceleration.

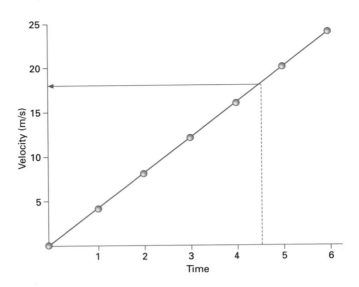

(b) The velocity at 4.5 seconds can be found as shown by drawing a line up to meet graph from 4.5 seconds. Answer = 18 m/s.

(c) The acceleration can be found by taking any two points on the graph.

Velocity at 0 seconds = 0 m/s
Velocity at 6 seconds = 24 m/s

$$\text{acceleration} = \frac{\text{change in velocity}}{\text{time}}$$

$$= \frac{24}{6} = 4\,\text{m/s}^2$$

Chapter 3
Force and Types of Force: Hooke's Law

Force is that which causes a body to move or change its velocity. Force is measured in newtons (N). There are many different kinds of force:

- Pushing or pulling.
- Weight (the pull of gravity on a body).
- Friction.

Gravity is a pulling force from the centre of the earth. It is important not to confuse weight and mass in physics.

Formula to link mass and weight:

$$weight = mass \times g$$

$$where\ g = acceleration\ due\ to\ gravity$$

Example: Find the weight of a person with a mass of 50 kg if the acceleration due to gravity is 10 m/s^2.

$$weight = mg$$

$$= 50 \times 10 = 500\ N$$

Friction is a force which prevents easy movement between two objects in contact. The rougher the two surfaces in contact, the greater the friction, e.g. sandpaper and timber.

Advantages of friction:

- Allows cars, bikes, etc. to stop.
- Allows grip so a person can walk, climb, etc.

Disadvantages of friction:

- Wear and tear of tyres, footwear, etc.
- Heating effect and loss of energy.

To reduce friction:

- Oil or grease the surface.
- Sand or polish the surface.

Experiment: Investigate the force of friction.

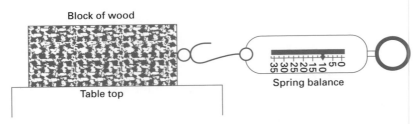

Block of wood

Spring balance

Table top

1. Attach a spring balance to a block of wood, as shown. A spring balance is used to measure force in newtons.
2. Note the reading on the spring balance as the block is about to move.
3. Attach some sandpaper to the base of the block and take the reading again as the block is about to move. The reading will be larger this time, as the friction is increased.
4. Repeat with oil on the base of the block and it will be noted that the reading for force is less, as oil reduces friction.

Forces occur in pairs. For every force, there is an equal and opposite force.

Example: Action and reaction: when a gun is fired, the gun recoils. The firing of the gun is the action and the recoil is the reaction.

Hooke's Law for a Spiral Spring

Hooke's law: The extension in a spiral spring is directly proportional to the force, provided the elastic limit of the spring is not exceeded.

Problem on Hooke's law: If a force of 5 N produces an extension of 15 cm, what extension would a 16 N force cause?

Solution: By Hooke's law, force is proportional to extension.

5 N produces a force of 15 cm.

$\Rightarrow$ 1 N produces a force of 3 cm.

$\Rightarrow$ 16 N produces a force of 48 cm.

Mandatory experiment: Prove Hooke's law.

1. Set up the apparatus as shown in the diagram.

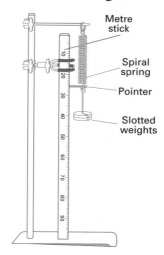

2. Add a slotted weight to make the spring taut.
3. Note the position of the pointer. This is the zero position.
4. Add different slotted weights and note the position of the pointer each time. Subtract the length at the zero position to find the extension.
5. Plot a graph of extension against force applied.
6. The graph is a straight line through the origin, proving that extension is proportional to the force and thus proving Hooke's law.

Graph for Hooke's Law

The following table of results from an experiment on Hooke's law shows readings of extension against force.

Extension (cm)	1	2	3	4	5	6
Force (N)	5	10	15	20	25	30

Plot a graph of the results on graph paper.

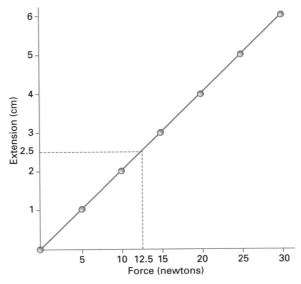

Using the graph, find the weight of a body producing an extension of 2.5 cm.

Solution: Draw a line across from 2.5 cm, as shown, to meet the graph. Then draw a vertical line down to meet the force axis. It is important to draw these lines to verify that the graph was used.

force = 12.5 N

The following points are important to note concerning the drawing of graphs in exam questions:

- Use graph paper.
- Label each axis and draw them in the correct position, as outlined in the question.
- Number the scale on each axis clearly.
- Show the points clearly and draw the line through the points.

Chapter 4
Work, Power and Energy

$$\boxed{\text{work} = \text{force} \times \text{distance}}$$

Work is done in physics when an object is moved a certain distance. Work is measured in Nm, or joules.

Example: Find the work done when a force of 50 N moves a body 20 m.

$$\text{work} = \text{force} \times \text{distance}$$
$$= 50 \times 20 = 1000 \text{ Nm (joules)}$$

Power is the rate of doing work: power = work ÷ time. Power is measured in watts or joules/second.

Example: A bulldozer moves a weight of 500 N a distance of 100 m in 5 seconds. Find (a) the work done (b) the power of the bulldozer.

Solution:

(a) work = force × distance = 500 × 100 = 50,000 joules (J)

(b) power = $\dfrac{\text{work}}{\text{time}} = \dfrac{50{,}000}{5}$ = 10,000 watts (W)

Types of Energy

Energy is the ability to do work. Therefore, energy and work have the same unit, joules.

Types of energy:

- **Potential energy:** Energy a body has due to its position or state. It is stored energy, e.g. energy in a coiled spring.
- **Kinetic energy:** Energy that a moving body has.
- **Heat energy:** In a hot air balloon, the heat energy causes the balloon to rise.

- **Light energy:** Such as in a solar-powered calculator.
- **Electrical energy:** Converted to heat in an electric kettle.
- **Sound energy:** Sound energy can cause a glass to break.
- **Chemical energy:** Energy from petrol makes a car move.
- **Nuclear energy:** Energy stored in the nucleus of atoms can be changed into electrical energy in a nuclear power plant.

Sources of Energy

What is the primary source of energy?
The sun is the primary source of energy, as most other types of energy can be traced back to it. It passes its light and heat energy to us in the form of radiation. For example, plants use light energy in photosynthesis to make food.
Non-renewable energy is energy that cannot be replaced. Examples are fossil fuels, i.e. fuels formed from the remains of dead plants and animals over very long periods of time, such as oil, coal, gas and turf.
Renewable energy is energy that can be replaced, such as solar, hydroelectric, wind and wave, as well as biomass energy (some plants produce oils which can be used to make fuels such as alcohols and methane gas) and geothermal energy (temperature under the earth's surface increases with depth and can be used to heat water in some places).

Nuclear energy: When the nucleus of large atoms such as uranium undergo fission (are split), large amounts of energy are released. This energy can be used in a nuclear power plant to produce electricity.

Advantages of nuclear energy:
- Source of electrical energy.
- Used in medicine to treat cancer.
- Used in the food industry to sterilise food.

Disadvantages of nuclear energy:
- Waste products are harmful to the environment.
- It is difficult to dispose of waste.
- Danger of nuclear accidents, e.g. Chernobyl.

Advantages and disadvantages of other energy sources:

Energy source	Advantages	Disadvantages
Wind	No pollution, renewable	Unreliable
Solar	No pollution, renewable	Difficult to store
Fossil fuel	Can be stored, relatively cheap	Causes pollution, non-renewable
Tidal	No pollution, renewable	Supply varies

Energy Conversions

The **law of conservation of energy** states that energy cannot be created or destroyed, but can be converted from one form to another.

Examples of energy conversions:

- An electric kettle converts electrical energy to heat energy.
- A car battery converts chemical energy to electrical energy.
- A radio converts electrical energy to sound energy.

Mandatory experiment: Convert chemical energy to electrical energy to heat energy.

1. Set up a circuit as follows:

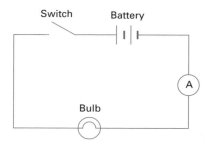

2. Turn on the switch. The bulb lights.
3. The experiment proves that chemical energy in the battery turns to electrical energy, making the current flow. This electrical energy is converted to light (and heat) energy in the bulb.

Mandatory experiment: Convert electrical energy to magnetic energy to kinetic energy.

1. Set up the following circuit.

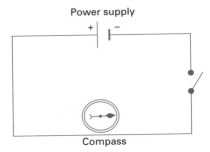

2. Place the plotting compass close to the length of wire used for the circuit.
3. Close the switch. The needle on the compass moves.
4. This proves that electrical energy in the circuit has been changed to magnetic energy in the compass. This magnetic energy has in turn been changed to kinetic energy in the movement of the needle.

Mandatory experiment: Convert light energy to electrical energy to kinetic energy.

1. Set up the circuit as follows:

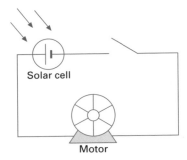

2. Shine a bright light onto the solar cell. The fan connected to the electric motor starts to spin. This proves that the solar energy from the lamp has been converted to electrical energy in the circuit. In turn, the electrical energy in the motor is then changed to kinetic energy when the fan moves.

Chapter 5
Weight and Turning Forces

Weight is the pull of gravity on a body. Weight is a force and is therefore measured in **newtons (N)**. As already noted, it is important not to confuse mass and weight.

Mass:
- The amount of matter in a body.
- Does not change.
- Measured in kilograms.

Weight:
- The pull of gravity on a body.
- Varies from place to place.
- Measured in newtons.

To convert mass into weight, use the formula

$$\text{weight} = \text{mass} \times \text{acceleration due to gravity} = mg$$

$$= \text{mass} \times 10 \text{ (approximate value of } g)$$

Example: Find the weight of a body of mass 200 g.

First convert mass to kg $\Rightarrow$ 200 g $= \dfrac{200}{1{,}000} = 0.2$ kg

$$\text{weight} = \text{mass} \times 10 = 0.2 \times 10 = 2 \text{ N}$$

Variation of Weight from Place to Place

The weight of a body on the moon is one-sixth the weight on the earth, as the gravity force on the moon is only one-sixth that of the earth. The weight of a body in outer space is zero (weightless), as there is no gravity.

Levers

A **lever** is any rigid body free to move about a point called a fulcrum.

Everyday applications of levers:

- A wheelbarrow enables easy movement of loads.
- A spanner enables us to apply a greater turning force to a stone, enabling us to move it.

Diagram of spanner working as a lever:

- Load is where force takes effect.
- Fulcrum is the turning point.
- Effort is where force is applied.

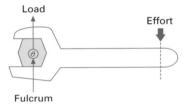

Moments and the Law of the Lever

The turning effect of a force is called the **moment**. It depends on:

- Force applied.
- The perpendicular distance to the fulcrum (point where the force is applied).

A moment of a force is defined as:

> moment = force × perpendicular distance to the fulcrum

Law of the lever: If a lever is balanced, the moment on the left is equal to the moment on the right.

Experiment: Prove the law of the lever.

1. Hang a metre stick from the 50 cm mark until it is balanced.
2. Hang a 15 N weight on one side of the metre stick and a 20 N weight on the other side. Move the weights until a point of balance is reached, as in the diagram.

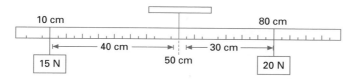

Moment on left (anticlockwise moment) = 15 × 40 = 600 Ncm

Moment on right (clockwise moment) = 20 × 30 = 600 Ncm

As the moment on the left = the moment on the right, the law has been proven.

Sample Problems on the Law of the Lever

Problem 1: Find the weight of an object using the law of the lever.

Example: Find the weight of the object X in the following experiment, where the lever is balanced.

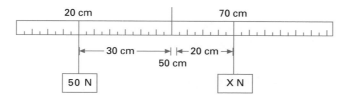

moment on left = moment on right

$$50 \times 30 = 20 \times X$$

$$X = \frac{1{,}500}{20} = 75 \text{ N}$$

Problem 2: Law of the lever.
This is a more difficult problem, where more than two weights are involved.

Example: Find the value of X in the following experiment where the lever is balanced.

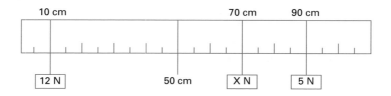

In this experiment, there is one moment on the left, but there are two separate moments on the right.

$$\text{moment on left} = 12 \times 0.4 = 4.8 \text{ Nm}$$

$$\text{moments on right} = X(0.2) + 5(0.4) = 0.2X + 2$$

$$\text{moment on left} = \text{moments on right}$$

$$0.2X + 2 = 4.8$$

$$0.2X = 2.8 \Rightarrow X = 14 \text{ N}$$

Centre of Gravity and Stability of Objects

The **centre of gravity** is the point in a body where all its weight acts.
A body is balanced if supported at its centre of gravity. For example, a rectangular sheet of cardboard can be supported where the diagonals meet.

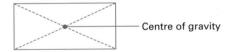

Experiment: Find the centre of gravity of an irregular sheet of cardboard (a lamina).

1. Hang the cardboard from a pin on a stand. It is important that the cardboard can swing freely.
2. Hang a plumbline from the pin and draw a vertical line on the cardboard along the plumbline.
3. Hang the cardboard from a different position and repeat step 2.

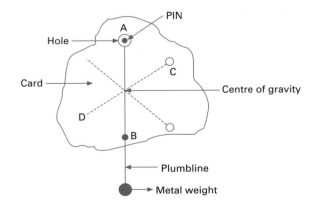

4. Again, repeat step 2 and draw a third line on the cardboard.
5. The centre of gravity is the point where the three lines meet.

Equilibrium and Stability of Objects

Equilibrium is the state of rest of a body.
The **stability** of an object depends on:

- The width of its base – the wider the base, the more stable the object.
- The position of its centre of gravity – the lower the centre of gravity, the more stable the object.

A stable design is achieved by widening the base and lowering the centre of gravity of a body. For example:

- A racing car has a wide base and low centre of gravity to prevent it from turning over at bends when travelling at high speeds.
- A double-decker bus would be more stable if more passengers stayed down on the lower deck, as this would mean that the centre of gravity is lower. The bus will topple over if its centre of gravity is outside the base, as shown in the diagram.

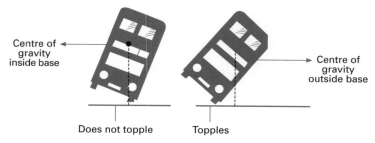

Centre of gravity inside base   Centre of gravity outside base

Does not topple   Topples

There are three states of equilibrium:

- **Stable equilibrium:** When the object is tilted, its centre of gravity is raised. Upon release, it goes back to its original position.

Stable equilibrium (CG = centre of gravity):

CG

- **Unstable equilibrium:** When an object is tilted, its centre of gravity is lowered and it takes up a new position when released.

  Unstable equilibrium: Topples over when moved.

- **Neutral equilibrium:** When an object is moved, its centre of gravity does not change position. When moved, it stays in neutral equilibrium in a new position.

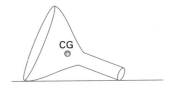

Chapter 6
Pressure

$$\boxed{\text{pressure} = \frac{\text{force}}{\text{area}}}$$

Pressure is the force per unit area.

Pressure is measured in N/m^2, or pascals.

The smaller the area, the greater the pressure for the same force.

Example: A person standing on one foot will sink further in soft ground than a person on two feet. Standing on one foot doubles your pressure.

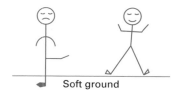

Soft ground

Find the pressure exerted by the following rectangular box if it exerts a force of 600 N on its side with dimensions 5 m by 4 m.

$$\text{pressure} = \frac{\text{force}}{\text{area}} = \frac{600}{4 \times 5} = 30 \, N/m^2$$

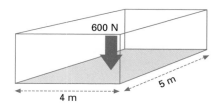

600 N

5 m

4 m

Pressure in Liquids

Liquid pressure increases with depth. This can be shown by putting three holes at different levels in a plastic bottle, as shown in the diagrams.

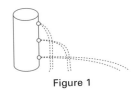

Figure 1

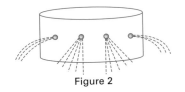

Figure 2

The greatest pressure is at the bottom, producing the strongest jet (see Figure 1).

Liquid pressure is the same in all directions. This can be achieved by placing holes at the same level in a plastic bottle of water and showing that the jets produced are of equal strength (see Figure 2).

Atmospheric Pressure

The band of gas surrounding the earth – the atmosphere – exerts a pressure called **atmospheric pressure**. This pressure is greatest on the surface of the earth but decreases as we go upwards.

Experiment: Show atmospheric pressure.

1. Fill a glass tumbler with water.
2. Place a sheet of strong paper or cardboard over the mouth of the glass and invert the glass.
3. Remove your hand. The water will not come out, as the atmospheric pressure acting upwards keeps the card in place.

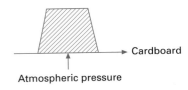

Cardboard

Atmospheric pressure

Experiment: Show that air has mass.

1. Find the mass of an empty balloon.
2. Blow up the balloon with air and tie it.
3. Find the mass of the balloon with air.

Result: The mass has increased, showing the air has mass.

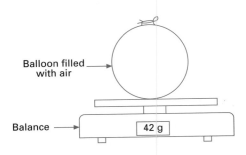

Balloon filled with air

Balance

42 g

Experiment: Show that air takes up space or volume.

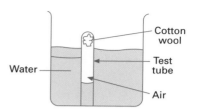

1. Place some cotton wool at the bottom of a test tube. Place the test tube upside down in a beaker of water, as shown in the diagram.

2. Remove the test tube from the water.

Results and conclusion: The cotton wool is dry, as the air did not allow the water to enter the test tube.

Barometers

A **barometer** is used to measure atmospheric pressure. There are two types of barometer: a mercury barometer and an aneroid barometer.

To make a **mercury barometer**, a long, thick-walled glass tube about 1 metre long is filled with mercury and is inverted into a dish of mercury. The level of the mercury falls, leaving a vacuum called Toricelli's vacuum.

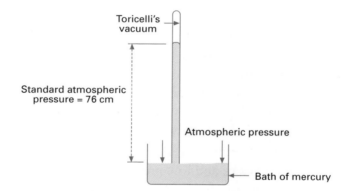

How does the mercury barometer work?

At standard atmospheric pressure, the height of mercury is 76 cm. If the pressure increases, the mercury is pushed up the tube and the reading will be higher. If the pressure is low, the height will drop below 76 cm.

An **aneroid barometer** is a metal box from which most of the air has been removed. The lid of the box moves up and down with changes in atmospheric pressure. The lid is connected to a pointer by a system of levers. The pointer moves on a scale showing high and low pressure.

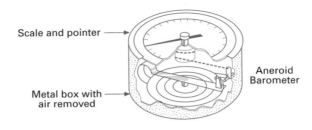

Scale and pointer →

Aneroid Barometer

Metal box with → air removed

Mercury barometer	Aneroid barometer
Very accurate	Not as accurate as mercury
Not convenient to use	Convenient to use, as it does not contain liquid and can be made quite small

Aneroid barometers are used to measure altitude. As one goes up, the atmospheric pressure decreases. Therefore, aneroid barometers are used in aeroplanes as altimeters to measure height.

Atmospheric Pressure and Weather

High pressure produces dry, calm, sunny weather. Why? When air is sinking, areas of high pressure, called anticyclones, are formed. If the pressure is high, water vapour is not allowed to rise and there will be dry, calm, sunny weather. Low pressure produces wet, windy, cloudy weather. Why? If the air is rising, areas of low pressure, called depressions, are created. If the pressure is low, the water vapour will rise and there will be wet, windy, cloudy weather.
A weather map shows lines of equal pressure, called **isobars**. These isobars are centred on areas of high pressure and low pressure. The wind blows along these lines, blowing clockwise around areas of high pressure and anticlockwise around areas of low pressure. When the lines are close together, there will be strong winds.

Chapter **7**
Heat and Heat Travel

Heat is a form of energy and therefore it can do work, e.g. a steam engine. Heat, like energy, is measured in **joules (J)**.

There are three methods of heat travel: conduction, convection and radiation.

Heat Travel by Conduction

Conduction is heat travel through a substance without the substance moving. The heat moves from particle to particle. For example, if you place a steel poker in a fire, the handle gets warm.

A **conductor** will allow heat to pass through it, e.g. copper is a good conductor of heat.

Insulators do not allow heat to pass through them, e.g. plastic is a good insulator. Tog value measures the insulation ability of a substance. The higher the tog value, the better the insulator.

Insulation in the Home

There are many ways of conserving heat energy by insulation in the home:

- Fibreglass in the attic prevents heat loss through the roof.
- Lagging jacket on hot water cylinder.
- Double-glazed windows.
- Aeroboard in the cavity of the walls.

Mandatory experiment: Compare the conductivity of different metals.

1. Set up the apparatus as shown in the diagram.
2. Stick pins to the ends of the rods with candle wax.
3. Place boiling water in the container.

Result and conclusion: The pin falls off the copper rod first, proving it is the best conductor.

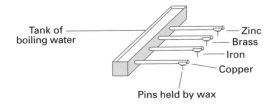

Tank of boiling water — Zinc — Brass — Iron — Copper

Pins held by wax

Heat Travel by Convection

Convection is the transfer of heat through a liquid or gas by the movement of the liquid or gas.

An everyday example of convection is that the element in an electric kettle is placed as low as possible so that full advantage can be taken of the convection currents in the water.

Mandatory experiment: Show convection currents in a liquid, e.g. water.

1. Place a crystal of purple potassium permanganate at the bottom of a beaker of cold water.

2. Heat the water. As the crystal dissolves in the water, it rises with the convection currents of water.

Result and conclusion: Soon all the liquid is a purple colour due to the convection currents in the water (see diagram).

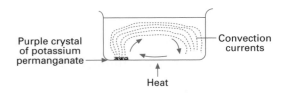

Purple crystal of potassium permanganate — Convection currents

Heat

Mandatory experiment: Show that water is a poor conductor of heat but a good convector of heat.

(A) Show water is a poor conductor of heat.

1. Set up the apparatus as shown in Figure 1.

2. Use a small weight to keep the ice cube at the bottom of the test tube.

3. Heat the water at the top of the test tube until it boils.

Result and conclusion: The ice will not melt, proving that water is a poor conductor of heat.

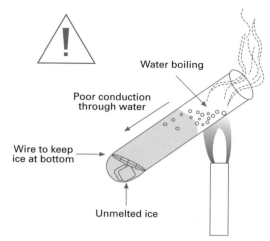

Water boiling

Poor conduction through water

Wire to keep ice at bottom

Unmelted ice

(B) Show that water is a good convector of heat.

1. Set up the apparatus as shown in Figure 2.
2. This time, heat the water from the bottom.

   Result and conclusion: The ice melts, proving that water convects heat well.

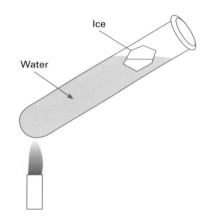

Ice

Water

Mandatory experiment: Show convection currents in air.

1. Place a small candle under chimney A (see diagram) and close the front door of the smoke box.
2. Hold a smoking taper over the other chimney B.

Result and conclusion: Smoke will appear out of chimney A due to a convection current of air travelling through the box.

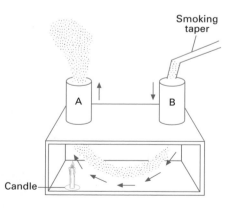

Smoking taper

A   B

Candle

Heat Transfer by Radiation

Radiation is heat travelling in rays.

Mandatory experiment: Show heat transfer by radiation from two different surfaces.

1. Fill two cans with an equal volume of boiling water.
2. One can has a dull black surface, while the other can has a shiny polished surface.
3. Place a thermometer in each can.
4. The temperature drops in each can, showing that heat is radiated from each.

Result and conclusion: The temperature in the black can drops faster, showing that black surfaces radiate heat better than bright surfaces.

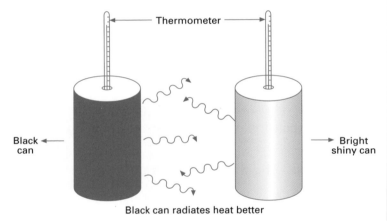

Black can radiates heat better

Effect of Heat on Solids, Liquids and Gases

Solids, liquids and gases expand when heated and contract when cooled.
Substances expand when heated as their molecules get heat energy and vibrate and move apart.
Gases expand better than liquids, as gas molecules are more separated and have greater movement when heated.
Likewise, liquid molecules expand better than solid molecules, as solid molecules are closer together than liquid molecules.

Mandatory experiment: Show that solids expand when heated and contract when cooled.

1. Pass the metal ball through the ring when cold.
2. Heat the ball strongly over a Bunsen burner.
3. The ball will not fit through the ring now, showing that expansion has taken place.
4. Cool the ball under the cold water tap.
5. The ball will now fit through the ring, as it has contracted when cooled.

Conclusion: Solids expand when heated and contract when cooled.

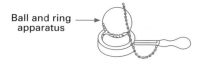
Ball and ring apparatus

Mandatory experiment: Show that liquids expand when heated and contract when cooled.

1. Fill a round-bottomed flask with water to which red dye has been added.
2. Fit a narrow glass tube to the flask and mark the level of the red-coloured water in the tube.
3. Heat the water. The level of water will rise quickly in the tube, showing that expansion of gases occurs easily upon heating.
4. Allow the flask to cool. The water will return to its former level upon contracting.

Water rises on heating

Conclusion: Liquids expand upon heating and contract when cooled.

Mandatory experiment: Show that gases expand upon heating and contract when cooled.

1. Set up the apparatus as shown.
2. Heat the flask gently with a Bunsen burner.

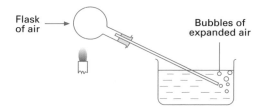
Flask of air

Bubbles of expanded air

3. Bubbles will be seen in the water, showing that expansion of the air in the tube has taken place.

4. If the flask is allowed to cool, the air will contract again and draw water into the flask.

Everyday Expansion of Solids, Liquids and Gases

Solids: A bimetallic strip.
Heat a bimetallic strip with a Bunsen burner and note that it bends upon heating. The reason for this is that it consists of two metals, copper and steel, and copper expands better upon heating and thus the strip bends, as shown in the diagram.

The bimetallic strip can be used in switches which turn circuits on and off, e.g. thermostats in electric kettles, electric fires, etc.

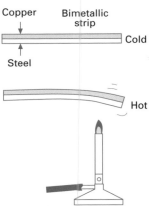

Copper   Bimetallic strip

Cold

Steel

Hot

Liquids: The expansion of mercury or alcohol in thermometers is an everyday use of expansion of liquids.

Gases: Hot air balloons are an everyday example of the expansion of gases.

Chapter 8
Temperature and Latent Heat

What is the difference between heat and temperature? **Heat** is a form of energy, but **temperature** is the degree of hotness of a body.

For example, a bucket of boiling water and a cup of boiling water are at the same temperature, but the bucket contains far more heat energy than the cup.

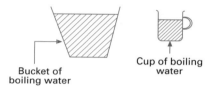

Bucket of boiling water

Cup of boiling water

Change of state:

- **Melting:** Heating of a solid to a liquid, e.g. ice to water.
- **Freezing:** Cooling of a liquid to a solid, e.g. water to ice.

Experiment: Show the melting and freezing of wax.

1. Set up the apparatus as shown.
2. Place a thermometer in the wax.
3. Note the temperature when the wax melts. This is the melting point of the wax.
4. Allow the wax to cool and it freezes back to a solid again.
5. This experiment demonstrates both melting and freezing.

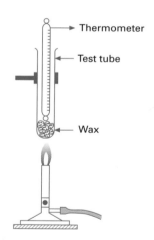

Thermometer

Test tube

Wax

Boiling point: The temperature at which a liquid changes to a gas.

Experiment: Find the boiling point of water and show the effect of pressure on the boiling point.

1. Set up the apparatus as shown.
2. Keep the clip open and heat the water until it boils.

3. Note that the temperature is 100°C. This is the normal boiling point of water.

4. Remove the Bunsen burner and close the clip on the rubber tube (see diagram). This creates a vacuum in the tube. Therefore, there is reduced pressure.

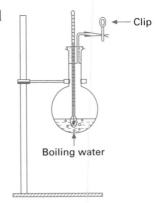

Boiling water

Result and conclusion: The water is seen to boil at a temperature lower than 100°C. Therefore, decreased pressure reduces the boiling point and increased pressure raises the boiling point.

Everyday Effect of Pressure on Boiling Point

As already noted, increased pressure raises the boiling point, e.g. a pressure cooker does not allow the steam to escape, therefore the pressure is higher. The water in the pressure cooker boils at a higher temperature of about 120°C, therefore the food cooks faster at this higher temperature.

Changes of state and latent heat:

- **Latent heat** is the heat used to change the state of a substance. It does not change the temperature.

- **Melting:** When a solid changes to a liquid, heat energy is used to separate the solid molecules into liquid molecules, e.g. ice molecules being heated to water molecules. The latent heat involved here is called latent heat of fusion.

- **Boiling:** Again, latent heat energy is needed to separate the liquid molecules further and break down any attractive forces between them, changing them into gas molecules. The latent heat involved here is called latent heat of vaporisation.

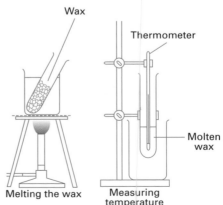

Experiment: Demonstrate latent heat by plotting a cooling curve.

1. Set up the apparatus as shown.

2. Boil the water in the beaker until the candle wax reaches a temperature of 90°C. Keep heating until all the wax has melted.

3. Turn off the Bunsen burner and remove the test tube of melted wax from the hot water. Read the temperature of the candle wax and start a stopwatch.

4. Allow the wax to cool and take the temperature. Take the temperature every minute for about ten minutes. At this stage, the candle wax will have frozen to a solid again.

Table of results:

Temperature (°C)	70	65	60	58	58	58	58	55	45	40
Time (minutes)	1	2	3	4	5	6	7	8	9	10

Draw a graph of the results.

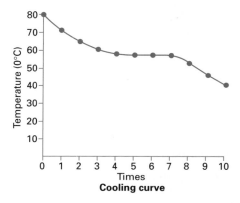

Cooling curve

The graph, called a cooling curve, will look like the one shown here. Note that at the level part of the curve there is no change in temperature, as this is where latent heat is given out when the liquid changes to a solid. The melting point of the wax is 58°C.

Chapter 9
Light

Light is a form of energy. It can do work, e.g. a solar-powered calculator.

Experiment: Show that light is a form of energy.

1. Shine a strong light on a Crooke's radiometer, as shown, and the metal vanes start to turn. The vanes turn as light energy is changed into heat energy, which in turn is changed into kinetic energy when the vanes start to move.

Crooke's
radiometer

Mandatory experiment: Show that light travels in straight lines.

1. Set up the apparatus as shown.
2. Ensure that the pinholes are in a straight line by pulling a piece of thread through them.
3. The light from the bulb can now be seen.
4. Move one of the pieces of cardboard out of line.

Result: The light can no longer be seen. Therefore, light travels in straight lines.

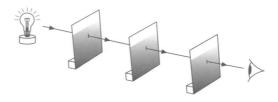

The formation of shadows also proves that light travels in a straight line.

Mandatory experiment: Show how shadows are formed.

1. Place a white sheet of cardboard about 1 metre from a lamp or torch.
2. Hold your hand between the torch and the light.

Result: A shadow is formed on the screen in the same shape as your hand.
If you move your hand closer to the light, the shadow gets bigger, as your hand is blocking more light.
Eclipses are another example of shadow formation.

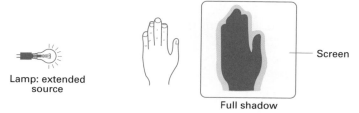

Lamp: extended source

Full shadow

Screen

In a solar eclipse, a shadow is formed on the earth when the moon comes between the sun and the earth.

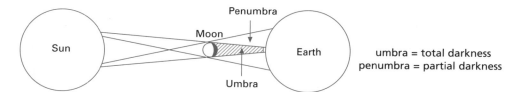

Sun

Moon

Penumbra

Umbra

Earth

umbra = total darkness
penumbra = partial darkness

Reflection of light occurs when light rays bounce off a surface.
A shiny polished surface, like a mirror, shows regular, orderly reflection where the angle of incidence is equal to the angle of reflection, as shown in the diagram.

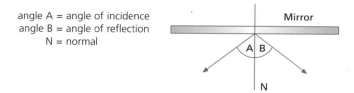

angle A = angle of incidence
angle B = angle of reflection
N = normal

Mirror

A B

N

Luminous and Non-luminous Bodies

Luminous bodies give out their own light, e.g. electric lamps, the sun.
Non-luminous bodies don't produce light, but rather reflect light from luminous bodies and therefore we can see them. Most objects are non-luminous.

Mandatory experiment: Show the reflection of light using a periscope.

1. Using a ray box, shine a ray of light into the top mirror in a periscope. The light reflects off the mirror, as shown in the diagram, and reflects off a

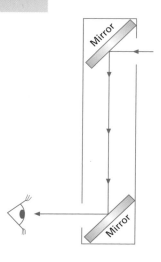

Mirror

Mirror

lower mirror and can be seen emerging parallel to the original ray. Note that both mirrors are angled at 45° for this to happen.

Refraction of Light

Refraction of light is the bending of light as it passes from one medium into another, e.g. light bends as it passes from air into water.

Experiment: Show the refraction of light.
1. Using a ray box, allow a ray of light to hit a glass block at an angle, as shown in the diagram.
2. As the ray passes through the glass, it bends *towards* the normal (perpendicular line to surface).
3. When the ray emerges from the glass, it bends *away* from the normal.
4. This experiment therefore shows the refraction of light.
5. Note that it also shows that when light is going from a less dense (air) to a more dense medium (glass), it bends in towards the normal and vice versa.

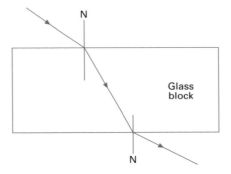

Everyday Examples of Refraction

- The bottom of a swimming pool appears higher up due to the refraction of the light rays as they come out of the water.
- Lenses are also an everyday example of refraction.

Lenses

A **lens** is a piece of glass or plastic with a curved surface.
There are two types of lenses: convex and concave.
A **convex,** or **converging, lens** gathers light rays to a point.

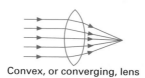

Convex, or converging, lens

Uses of convex lenses:

- A magnifying glass is an example of a use of a convex lens. It uses refraction to produce a magnified image of an object.
- Convex lenses are also used in spectacles to correct long-sightedness, i.e. a defect of the eye where only far-away objects can be seen.
- They are also used in microscopes, cameras and telescopes.

A **concave,** or **diverging, lens** spreads out light rays.

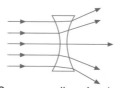

Concave, or diverging, lens

Uses of concave lenses:

- Concave lenses are used in spectacles to cure short-sightedness, i.e. where only objects close by can be seen.

Dispersion of Light

Dispersion of light is the breaking up of white light into its spectrum of colours. The colours that make up the spectrum of white light are red, orange, yellow, green, blue, indigo and violet.

Experiment: Show the dispersion of white light into its colours.

1. Using a ray box and a slit, allow a narrow beam of light to strike a glass prism.

2. Allow the dispersed light to hit a screen. A spectrum of the colours in white light is obtained, with red bent the least and violet bent the most.

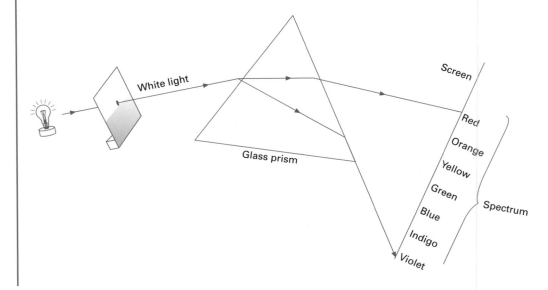

Chapter 10
Sound

Sound is a form of energy and is caused by vibrations of a medium such as a solid, liquid or gas, e.g. when plucked, the strings of a guitar cause vibrations in the air, which in turn vibrate our eardrum and our brain detects this as sound.

Experiment: Show that sound is a form of energy and is produced by vibrations.

1. Place a non-vibrating tuning fork beside a polystyrene ball. The ball does not move.
2. Hit the tuning fork off the bench and place it beside the ball again, as shown in the diagram.

Result and conclusion: This time, the ball moves, as the vibrating tuning fork produces sound energy, which is converted to kinetic energy of the moving ball.

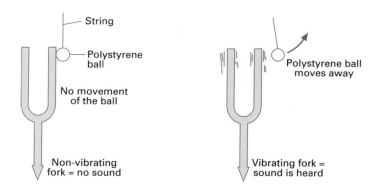

String
Polystyrene ball
No movement of the ball
Non-vibrating fork = no sound

Polystyrene ball moves away
Vibrating fork = sound is heard

Experiment: Show that sound needs a medium to travel.

1. Set up the apparatus as shown in the diagram.
2. Turn on the bell. Its sound can be heard clearly when there is air in the bell jar.
3. Remove air from the bell jar using a vacuum pump.

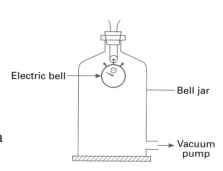

Electric bell
Bell jar
Vacuum pump

4. The sound cannot now be heard, proving that sound needs a medium (in this case, air) to travel.

Reflection of Sound

The **reflection of sound** is where sound waves bounce off a surface.
The formation of an echo is an example of sound bouncing off a surface. For example, if a person stands 100 m from a large wall and shouts loudly, the sound waves travel to the wall, bounce off and come back and can be heard again. This idea can be used to get an approximate value for the speed of sound.

Problem: A person stands 340 m from a vertical wall. He shouts loudly. It takes 2 seconds for the sound to return using a stopwatch. Find the speed of sound.

$$\text{speed} = \frac{\text{distance to and from wall}}{\text{time taken}} = \frac{680}{2} = 340 \text{ m/s}$$

Speed of Sound and Light

Light travels faster than sound and this is proved by the fact that we see lightning before we hear thunder, even though they both happen at the same time.
Ultrasounds are an example of the reflection of sound. Ultrasound is a high-frequency sound which cannot be heard by the human ear.
Ultrasound echoes are used by ships to determine the depth of the sea below them. The ship emits an ultrasound pulse and notes the time taken for the pulse

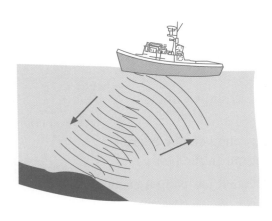

to return. The distance can be calculated using the formula distance = speed ×
time.
In medicine, ultrasound is used to view internal organs in the body of a
developing baby in the womb, as it is much safer than X-rays.

Experiment: Show the reflection of sound.

1. Set up the apparatus as shown in the diagram.
2. Place the two long cardboard tubes, A and B, in the same horizontal plane.
    Move tube B until the clicking of the clock is heard. The sound is heard the
    loudest when angle A = angle B.

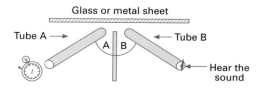

Loudness of Sound and Hearing Protection

The **decibel (dB)** is the unit used to compare the loudness of sounds.
Loudness of sounds can be measured using a sound level meter. The zero value is
the lowest sound that can be heard by the human ear and is called the threshold
of hearing.
As the decibel level rises, the danger of hearing damage increases. Regular
exposure to sounds above 70 decibels can be harmful if ear protection is not
used. Sound above 115 decibels can cause permanent damage to the human ear.
People working in noisy environments, e.g. industry or rock concerts, should use
ear protection.

Chapter 11
Magnetism

Properties of Magnets

- They attract iron, steel, nickel and cobalt.
- They have two centres of attraction, called poles, namely the north pole and the south pole.
- Like poles repel and unlike poles attract.
- When hanging freely, magnets point in a north-south direction.

Experiment: Show that like poles repel and unlike poles attract.

1. Suspend a magnet using a retort stand and thread, as shown in the diagram.
2. Bring another bar magnet near it so that the north poles are facing each other.
3. The magnets will be seen to move apart.
4. If a north pole was suspended near a south pole, they would move towards each other.

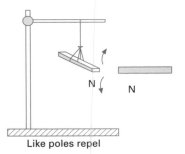

Like poles repel

Conclusion: Like poles repel and unlike poles attract.

The Magnetic Compass – the Earth's Magnetic Field

A **magnetic compass** is a small needle-like magnet balanced on a thin spindle. It is free to rotate and points in a north-south direction and therefore can be used in navigation.

The earth itself acts like a giant magnet, with its south pole in the geographical north and its north pole in the geographical south.

Thus, the magnetic compass will always point north, as it is attracted to the south pole of the earth's magnet.

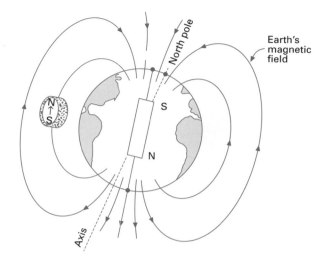

Magnetic Field

The **magnetic field** is the area around a magnet where a force is felt. The lines of force of a magnetic field run from the north pole to the south pole.

Experiment: Plot the magnetic field around a bar magnet.

1. Place a bar magnet on a sheet of paper.
2. Place a plotting compass at the north pole and mark the direction of north.
3. Replace the plotting compass ahead of this point and again mark the direction of north.
4. Repeat this process until the south pole is reached.

5. Join the dots to create a line of force of the magnetic field.
6. Repeat for a line of force below the magnet.

The result is as shown in the following diagrams.

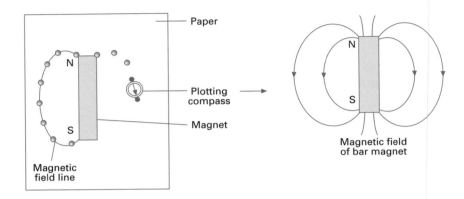

Uses of magnets:

- To keep doors of presses closed.
- In electric motors.
- In other electrical appliances such as computers, telephones, etc.

Storing Bar Magnets

If magnets are not stored properly, they lose their magnetism. Bar magnets are stored in pairs with unlike poles facing each other and iron pieces called sleepers at each end.

Chapter **12**
Static Electricity

Static electricity is electricity that does not move. It is a build-up of electric charge and can be produced by friction.

Experiment: Demonstrate the production of static electricity by friction.

1. Rub a plastic biro in your hair or your jumper.
2. Hold it near some small pieces of paper.

Result and conclusion: The paper is attracted to the biro due to static electricity on the plastic biro.

Biro charged with static electricity
attracts pieces of paper

Charging Rods Positively and Negatively

If a polythene rod is rubbed with a woollen cloth, it removes electrons from the cloth, giving it a negative charge as electrons are negative. Therefore, a body becomes **negatively charged** if it gains electrons.

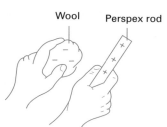

If a Perspex rod is rubbed with a woollen cloth, it loses electrons to the cloth, giving it a positive charge, and the cloth gets a negative charge. Therefore, a body becomes **positively charged** if it loses electrons.

Experiment: Show that like charges repel.

1. Suspend a negatively charged polythene rod from a retort stand using some thread.
2. Bring another negatively charged polythene rod near it.

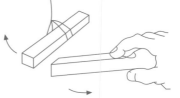

Result and conclusion: The suspended rod will move away. Therefore, like charges repel.

Experiment: Show that unlike charges attract.

1. Suspend a negative (polythene) rod from a retort stand.
2. Bring a positive (Perspex) rod close to the negative rod.

Unlike charges attract

Result and conclusion: The rods will be seen to attract. Therefore, unlike charges attract.

Conductors and Insulators of Electricity

A **conductor** allows electricity to flow through it, e.g. copper or any metal. An **insulator** does not allow electricity to flow through it, e.g. plastic.

Earthing

Earthing means connecting an object to earth using a conductor so that the object loses its charge to earth.

For example, buildings are often fitted with a lightning conductor. This consists of a metal spike on top of the building which is attached to a copper strip that connects with a metal buried in the ground. Therefore, it collects the static electricity from the lightning and conducts it away to earth, thus protecting the building.

Experiment: Show earthing.

1. Charge two polythene rods with a negative charge using a woollen cloth.
2. Suspend them from retort stands near each other, as in the previous experiment, and note that they repel.

3. Now touch each rod with a piece of metal, e.g. copper.

Result and conclusion: The rods no longer repel. The copper earthed the two rods, removing their charge so that they no longer repel.

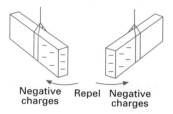

Negative   Repel Negative
charges   charges

Chapter 13
Current Electricity

An **electric current** is a flow of electrons through a substance.
Conductors, e.g. metals, allow electricity to flow through them, whereas
insulators, e.g. plastic, do not allow electricity to flow through them.

Mandatory experiment: Test for conductors and insulators.

1. Set up the circuit as shown.
2. Place a conductor such as a piece of copper in the gap left for the test
    material. Result: The bulb will light, proving that copper is a conductor.
3. Now place a piece of plastic in the gap. Result: This time the bulb will not
    light, proving that plastic is an insulator.

Conclusion: Conductors allow electricity to flow through them but insulators do
not.

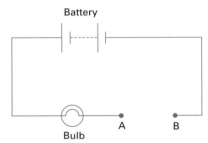

Place the test material between A and B

It is important to note from this experiment that an electric current will not flow
unless a circuit is complete.

Potential Difference

Potential difference is the difference in electrical pressure between the positive
and negative terminals of a battery. This causes electrons to flow around a circuit
from the negative to the positive terminal.

B convention, however, the direction of the current is taken as going from the positive to the negative terminals.

Potential difference (voltage) is measured in volts and is measured by a voltmeter.

The bigger the potential difference (the bigger the voltage of the battery), the greater the current that will flow.

Current

Current is the flow of electrons in a circuit. Current is measured in amps (A) and is measured by an ammeter.

Resistance

Resistance is the ability of a substance to slow down the flow of current in a circuit. It is measured in ohms (Ω) and is measured by an ohmmeter.

An example of resistance is the element in an electric kettle that gets hot when it resists the flow of electricity through it, converting electrical energy to heat energy.

The greater the resistance of a circuit, the smaller the current that flows.

Ohm's Law Relating Voltage, Current and Resistance

Ohm's law states that at constant temperature, the voltage (V) is always proportional to the current (I) in a circuit.

Formula for Ohm's law: $\dfrac{V}{I} = R$

where V = voltage, I = current and R = resistance.

For problems on Ohm's law, use this handy triangle:

From the triangle: $V = I \times R$, $\dfrac{V}{I} = R$ and $I = \dfrac{V}{R}$

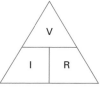

The phrase 'Very Important Result' will help you remember this formula.

Important Circuit Symbols

| Cell | Battery | Switch | Filament lamp | Fuse | Ammeter |

| Variable resistor | | Earth | Signal lamp | Resistor | Voltmeter |

Problems on Ohm's Law

Problem 1: Find the current flowing in the circuit shown in the diagram.

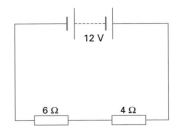

Resistors in series: Total $R = R_1 + R_2$

The total resistance here is $6 + 4 = 10\ \Omega$

From Ohm's law: $I = \dfrac{V}{R} = \dfrac{12}{10} = 1.2\ \text{A (amps)}$

Problem 2: Find the potential difference in the following circuit if the reading on the meter Y is 0.5. What is meter X called? What is meter Y called?

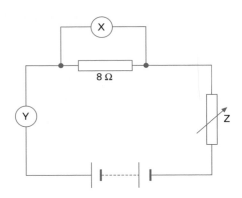

Solution: Meter Y is called the ammeter and reads the current. Therefore, current = 0.5 A.

Meter X is called the voltmeter and reads the voltage. To calculate the voltage, use Ohm's law.

$$V = I \times R$$

$$V = 0.5 \times 8 = 4 \text{ V (volts)}$$

Mandatory experiment: Prove Ohm's law.

1. Set up the circuit as shown in the diagram.

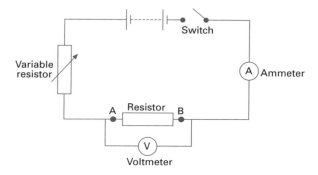

2. Close the switch and allow the current to flow.
3. Take the reading for current on the ammeter and voltage on the voltmeter.
4. Adjust the variable resistor and take different readings of voltage and current.

Results and conclusion: Plot a graph of voltage against current and the result is a straight line. This proves that voltage is directly proportional to current and therefore proves Ohm's law.

Example of Ohm's Law Graph

In an experiment to verify Ohm's law, the following readings were taken.

Voltage	0	4	8	12	16	20
Current	0	1	2	3	4	5

(a) Use the table to draw a graph of voltage against current, putting current on the horizontal axis. Explain how the graph proves Ohm's law.

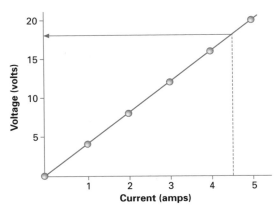

(b) Use the graph to calculate the resistance of the resistor used in this experiment.

(c) The graph is a straight line through the origin, proving that voltage is proportional to current and therefore proving Ohm's law.

(d) To calculate resistance, use Ohm's law and two readings from the graph:

$$R = \frac{V}{I} = \frac{18}{4.5} = 4 \, \Omega$$

Series and Parallel Circuits

Series circuit

If bulbs or resistors are connected in series, it means they are connected one after the other.

In a series circuit with three bulbs, as shown in the diagram, the resistance is increased and therefore the current is reduced. Therefore, the bulbs will be dimmer than if there was one or two bulbs in the circuit.

Also, if one bulb 'blows' (its filament burns out), the other bulbs will not work, as there is a break in the circuit.

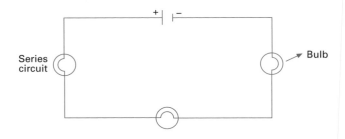

Parallel circuits

Bulbs connected in parallel are connected side by side.

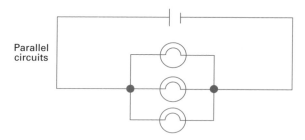

Parallel
circuits

Unlike a series circuit, if one bulb is disconnected, the other bulbs will still work, as there is an alternative pathway for the current to flow through. Also, the bulbs are brighter, as the total resistance in the circuit is less. Parallel circuits are therefore used in houses for the above reasons.

Effects of an Electric Current

There are three effects of an electric current: heating, magnetic and chemical.

Experiment: Show the heating effect of an electric current.
1. Set up the circuit as shown in the diagram.
2. Switch on the current.
3. The bulb lights, proving that the electric current has a heating effect on the filament, causing it to light.

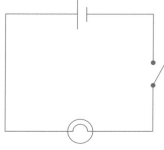

Experiment: Show the magnetic effect of an electric current.
1. Set up the circuit as shown in the diagram.
2. Switch on the current.
3. The compass needle on the compass moves, proving that an electric current has a magnetic effect.

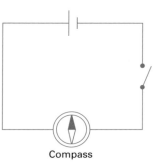

Compass

Experiment: Show that an electric current has a chemical effect.

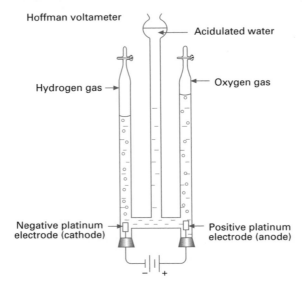

1. Set up the Hoffmann voltameter as shown and fill it with water to which some sulphuric acid has been added.
2. The sulphuric acid provides ions, which carry the current.
3. The electrodes are made of platinum or graphite.
4. Switch on the current and note that hydrogen gas collects at the negative electrode.
5. Oxygen gas collects at the positive electrode.
6. This experiment shows that water can be split into hydrogen and oxygen by electrolysis, i.e. the chemical change brought about by an electric current.

Chapter **14**
Electricity in the Home

Types of Circuit in the Home

Ring main circuit

As shown in the diagram, the live, neutral and earth wires form a ring. The live wire is protected by a fuse. Sockets can be tapped off at different points along the ring. The advantages of this type of circuit are that:

- It uses less current, as it splits the current.
- If one socket malfunctions, the others still work.

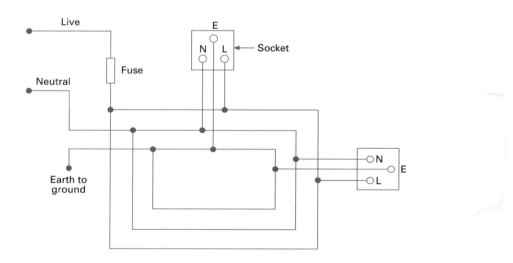

Lighting circuit

Lights are connected in parallel so that if one fails, the others still work.

Safety Devices in the Home

- **Fuse:** A fuse contains a thin piece of wire that melts and breaks the circuit if too large a current flows through it. It is important to use the right fuse for the right appliance or circuit. The correct fuse to use should be higher than the current that normally flows through the appliance but as close as possible to it. For example, low-power items such as televisions and bedside lamps are fitted with 3 A fuses, as they use currents that are less than this.

- **Circuit breakers:** These are switches with a bimetallic strip fitted which switch off the current if they heat up due to an electrical fault. Circuit breakers are better than fuses in that they don't have to be replaced, just switched on again.

- **Earth wire:** This is a wire that runs to a metal plate buried in the ground. If a fault develops in a metal appliance, the earth wire provides an easy path for the current to flow through rather than giving a huge shock to a person touching the appliance.

Plugs

Wiring a household plug

The brown, or live, wire is connected to the fuse, as shown. The blue, or neutral, wire is connected to the left terminal. The earth, or green and yellow, wire is connected to the top terminal.

L = live
N = neutral
E = earth

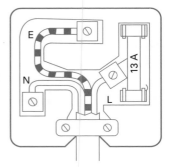

Electric power

The watt (W) is the unit of electric power. A 100 W bulb uses more power than a 60 W bulb. A 60 W bulb converts 60 joules of electrical energy into heat and light energy per second.

$$\boxed{\text{electric power} = \text{voltage} \times \text{current}}$$

Problem 1: An electric kettle has a power rating of 2400 W. The ESB provides 220 V to households. Find the current used by an electric kettle and state whether a 10 A or 13 A fuse should be used for it.

Solution:

$$\text{electric power} = \text{voltage} \times \text{current}$$

$$2400 = (220)I$$

$$I = 10.9 \text{ A}$$

Therefore, a 13 A fuse should be used.

The unit of power used by the ESB is the kilowatt hour. A kilowatt hour is when a kilowatt of electricity is used for one hour.

Find the cost of using a 100 W bulb for five hours a day for fifty days at 15c per unit.

First change to kilowatts:

$$100 \text{ W} = 0.1 \text{ kW}$$

$$0.1 \text{ kW for 5 hours} = 0.5 \text{ kW hours}$$

$$0.5 \text{ kW hours for 50 days} = 25 \text{ kW hours}$$

$$25 \text{ kW hours} = 25 \text{ units}$$

$$\text{cost} = 25 \times 0.15 = €3.75$$

Direct Current and Alternating Current

Direct current flows in one direction only, but **alternating current** can change its direction 100 times per second. Direct current comes from a battery where the current flows in one direction from positive to negative.

The ESB supplies alternating current to households, as it is easier to produce and cheaper to distribute. The AC voltage is supplied by the ESB at 220 V. In a house, lights or heating elements work on alternating current. However, electrical appliances like televisions and computers work on direct current. They contain a device called a rectifier which converts alternating current to direct current. In addition, transformers are needed to reduce the voltage from 220 V to the voltage of the appliance.

Chapter 15
Electronics

Electronics is the careful and exact control of very small electric currents.

Function of Diodes and Their Uses

A **diode** is an electrical device that allows current to flow in one direction only.

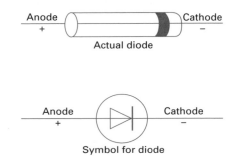

The current flows in the direction of the arrow. The current will only flow if the arrow points to the negative terminal of the battery, as shown above. In this position, the diode is said to be in forward bias.

Experiment: Show the action of a diode.

1. Set up the following circuits.

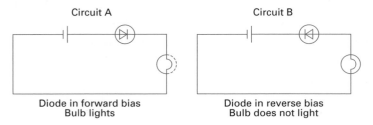

2. In circuit A, the diode is in forward bias, i.e. the positive terminal of the battery is connected to the positive terminal of the diode, thus it will allow current to flow through it, as the 'arrow' in its symbol suggests.

3. Therefore, when the current is switched on with the diode in forward bias, the bulb will now light.

4. However, if the direction of the diode is reversed, i.e. the positive terminal of the battery is connected to the negative terminal of the diode, as in circuit B, the bulb will not light as the diode is in reverse bias.

Function of Diodes

Diodes can be used to change alternating current into direct current. Many electronic devices such as radios and computers can only use low-voltage direct current, as already mentioned. They contain AC adaptors built into them, which in turn contain:

- A transformer to reduce the voltage from 220 V to about 12 V.
- A diode rectifier, which converts alternating current (AC) to direct current (DC), as the appliance can only use DC.

Light-Emitting Diodes (LEDs)

An **LED** is a diode that will give out light when a current flows through it. The following circuit shows an LED in action.

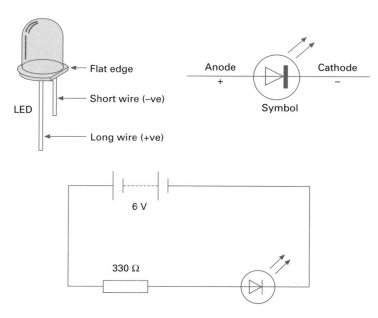

An LED only uses very small currents. Too big a current will damage the diode, therefore a large resistance is placed in series with it as it reduces the current in the circuit.

Use of LEDs

LEDs are available in red, green or yellow and are used in electronic displays, e.g. electronic clocks. The advantage of LEDs is that they use far less current than a bulb and are therefore cheaper and also last a lot longer than bulbs.

Experiment: Use an LED to test for the positive and negative terminal of a battery.

1. Set up the circuit as shown in the diagram.

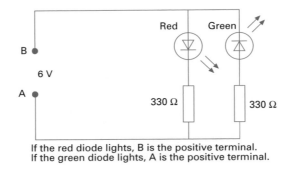

If the red diode lights, B is the positive terminal.
If the green diode lights, A is the positive terminal.

2. Connect the two LEDs in opposite directions.
3. Connect the battery to be tested between A and B.
4. If B is the positive terminal, then the red LED will light, as it is in forward bias. However, if the green LED lights, then A is the positive terminal, as the green LED is now in forward bias.

Light-Dependent Resistor (LDR)

An **LDR** is a resistor whose resistance depends on the amount of light falling on it. When light falls on an LDR, its resistance decreases.

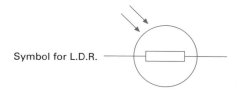

Symbol for L.D.R.

Experiment: Show the action of an LDR.

1. Set up the circuit as shown in the diagram.

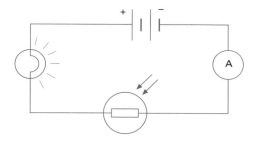

2. Using a bench lamp, allow strong light to shine on the LDR.

    The bulb in the circuit lights brightly as the resistance of the LDR is low when light falls on it, allowing more current to flow.

3. Now move the bench lamp further away from the LDR, which reduces the amount of light falling on the LDR. The bulb is only dimly lit, as less current flows in the circuit, as the resistance of the LDR increases in dim light.

Uses of LDRs

*   LDRs are used in street lighting, allowing lights to come on when daylight fades.
*   They are also used in light meters for cameras.

Experiment: Show that the resistance of an LDR changes in different degrees of brightness.

1. Set up the following circuit with an ohmmeter that measures resistance and an LDR connected to it.

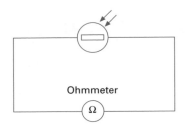

Ohmmeter

Ω

2. Turn on a bench lamp and move it close to the LDR. The resistance is low on the ohmmeter.

3. Move the bench lamp gradually away from the LDR.

Conclusion: It will be noted that the resistance increases as less and less low is shined on the LDR from the lamp. The greater the light intensity, the lower the resistance on the LDR.

CHEMISTRY

Chapter **16**
States of Matter and Elements

Chemistry is the study of what different substances are made of and how to change one substance into another. All the different substances can be called matter and there are three states of matter: **solid, liquid** and **gas**.

Differences Between the Three States of Matter

Solid	Liquid	Gas
Fixed shape	No fixed shape	No fixed shape
Does not flow	Does flow	Does flow
Strong forces between particles	Weak forces between particles	Very weak forces between particles

General Structure of Solids, Liquids and Gases

Matter is composed of tiny particles which may be **atoms** or **molecules**. The particles in a solid are held closely together in a rigid structure, which explains why they cannot flow.

The particles in a liquid are able to move around each other as the forces of attraction between them are weak. The particles in a gas have completely free movement and are well separated, as shown in the diagram.

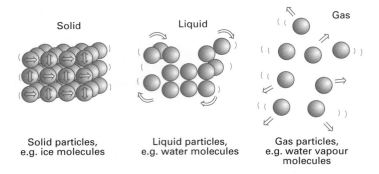

Solid

Liquid

Gas

Solid particles,
e.g. ice molecules

Liquid particles,
e.g. water molecules

Gas particles,
e.g. water vapour
molecules

Change of State

- **Melting point:** Temperature at which a solid is changed to a liquid, e.g. ice to water. The solid ice molecules get heat energy and start moving about and separate to become liquid molecules.
- **Boiling point:** Temperature at which a liquid changes to a gas, e.g. water to water vapour. The liquid molecules get more energy from heat and separate further into gas molecules.

Elements

- **Elements** are substances that cannot be made simpler, e.g. carbon is composed only of carbon atoms. It is found as graphite in pencils.
- An **atom** is the smallest part of an element that still retains the properties of that element, e.g. a carbon atom.
- A **molecule** is the smallest part of an element or compound that can exist on its own, e.g. an oxygen molecule (O_2) is the smallest part of oxygen gas. It consists of two oxygen atoms bonded together.

The First Twenty Elements

Element	Symbol	State
Hydrogen	H	Gas
Helium	He	Gas
Lithium	Li	Solid metal

Beryllium	Be	Solid metal
Boron	B	Solid non-metal
Carbon	C	Solid non-metal
Nitrogen	N	Gas
Oxygen	O	Gas
Fluorine	F	Gas
Neon	Ne	Gas
Sodium	Na	Solid metal
Magnesium	Mg	Solid metal
Aluminium	Al	Solid metal
Silicon	Si	Solid non-metal
Phosphorous	P	Solid non-metal
Sulphur	S	Solid non-metal
Chlorine	Cl	Gas
Argon	Ar	Gas
Potassium	K	Solid metal
Calcium	Ca	Solid metal

Commonly Known Metallic Elements and Their Uses

Element (metal)	Appearance	Use
Copper (Cu)	Reddish brown	Electric wires
Iron (Fe)	Silver grey	Ships, cars, etc.
Silver (Ag)	Bright grey	Jewellery
Gold (Au)	Yellow	Jewellery
Lead (Pb)	Grey	Batteries
Zinc (Zn)	Grey	Batteries
Aluminium (Al)	Grey	Windows

Commonly Known Non-Metallic Elements and Their Uses

Element (non-metal)	Appearance	Use
Carbon (C)	Black solid	Charcoal for fuel
Sulphur (S)	Yellow solid	Matches and fireworks
Oxygen (O_2)	Colourless gas	Welding and breathing
Hydrogen (H_2)	Colourless gas	Rocket fuel

Chapter 17
Compounds and Mixtures

A **compound** is the chemical union of two or more elements.

Experiment: Make the solid compound iron sulphide from the elements iron and sulphur.

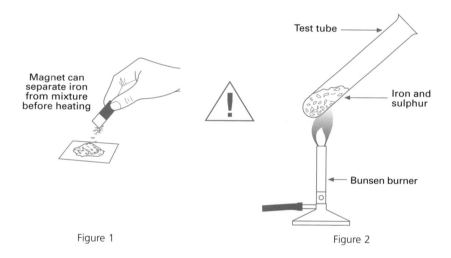

Figure 1

Figure 2

1. Mix some iron filings (small pieces of iron) and sulphur on filter paper.
2. Using a magnet, we can easily separate the mixture, as shown in Figure 1. The iron filings are grey in colour and the sulphur is yellow.
3. Now heat the mixture in a test tube in a fume cupboard, as shown in Figure 2.

Result and conclusion: A black solid is formed upon heating. If a magnet is now brought near this black solid, the iron can no longer be separated. This proves that a new compound, iron sulphide, has been formed that has properties different from the original mixture.

The reaction is: $\underset{\text{iron}}{\text{Fe}} + \underset{\text{sulphur}}{\text{S}} \rightarrow \underset{\text{iron sulphide}}{\text{FeS}}$

Chemical Change

The above experiment is an example of a **chemical change**, where a new substance is formed. Other examples of chemical changes are burning paper and rusting iron.

Physical Change

A **physical change** is where no new substance is formed, e.g. cutting paper, melting ice.

Other Compounds

An example of a liquid compound is water (H_2O). An example of a gaseous compound is carbon dioxide (CO_2).

Mixtures

A **mixture** is formed when two or more substances are physically combined, e.g. salt and water.

Differences between Compounds and Mixtures

Compound, e.g. water (H_2O)	Mixture, e.g. salty water
Chemically combined	Physically combined
Hard to separate	Easy to separate
Fixed make-up, e.g. water has two hydrogen atoms and one oxygen atom	Variable make-up, e.g. the amount of salt can vary in salty water

Separation of Mixtures

Different methods of separation depend on the type of mixture.

- **Filtration:** Used to separate an insoluble solid from a liquid, e.g. sand and water. Filter paper traps the large sand particles and the smaller water molecules pass through the tiny holes in the filter paper.

- **Evaporation:** Used to separate a soluble solid from a liquid by heating the liquid to a gas, leaving the solid behind, e.g. separating salt and water.

- **Distillation:** Evaporation followed by condensation. Used to separate two liquids with different boiling points, e.g. alcohol and water.

- **Chromatography:** Used to separate small amounts of dissolved substances in a mixture, e.g. paper chromatography can be used to separate the dyes in ink.

- **Crystallisation:** Solid crystals can be separated from a hot saturated solution when it is allowed to cool, e.g. copper sulphate crystals from a copper sulphate solution.

Mandatory experiment: Separate a mixture of sand and water by filtration. This is an example of a mixture of a solid and a liquid where the solid does not dissolve.

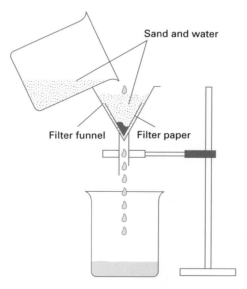

1. Set up the filtration apparatus as shown in the diagram.
2. Pour the mixture of sand and water into the filter funnel fitted with filter paper.

3. The water is collected in a beaker below.

Result: The water passes through the fine pores in the filter paper but the sand particles cannot, as they are too big. Therefore, sand and water are separated.

Mandatory experiment: Separate a mixture of sand and salt.
This is an example of separating a mixture of two solids, one of which dissolves in water, i.e. salt, and one of which does not dissolve, i.e. sand.

1. The sand and salt are first added to water in a beaker. The salt dissolves but the sand does not.
2. The sand is filtered using a filter funnel and paper, as shown in Figure 1.
3. The salty water that passes through the funnel is collected in an evaporating dish.
4. The water is evaporated, as shown in Figure 2. The salt remains in the dish. Thus, we have separated sand and salt.

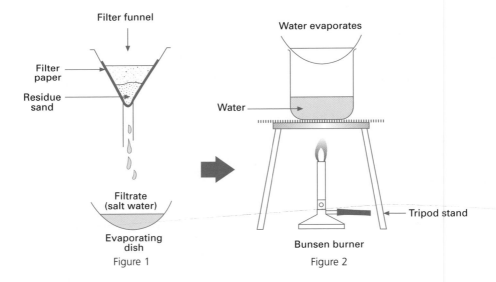

Figure 1

Figure 2

Experiment: Separate two immiscible liquids, i.e. liquids that do not mix, such as oil and water.

1. Pour a mixture of oil and water into a separating funnel.
2. The oil floats on top of the water.
3. The tap is opened and the water is released into a beaker below. The tap is then closed. We have thus separated oil and water.

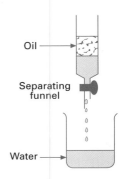

Mandatory experiment: Separate two miscible liquids, i.e. liquids that do mix, such as alcohol and water, by distillation.

Distillation is used here, i.e. separating mixtures by boiling and then condensing.

1. Set up the apparatus as shown in the diagram.

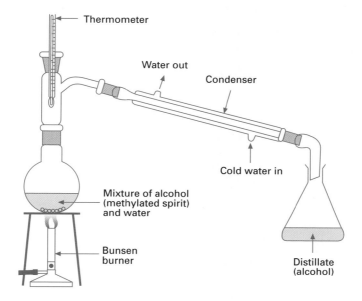

2. The mixture is heated to 78°C, which is the boiling point of alcohol. The alcohol vapour is cooled back to a liquid in the Liebig condenser and collected in the beaker. (Condensation is the term used to describe the cooling of a gas vapour into a liquid.)

3. The water remains in the flask, as it has a higher boiling point of 100°C.

Result: Alcohol and water have been separated. The alcohol collected is called the distillate.

Use of Distillation

The above technique is used in the brewing industry to produce beers, wines and whiskey.

Mandatory experiment: Separate the dyes in ink using paper chromatography. Chromatography is a method of separation where a liquid travels along a medium such as paper and separates substances in a mixture by carrying them different distances.

1. Place a concentrated drop of black fountain pen ink about 5 cm from the end of a strip of chromatography paper.
2. Hang the strip of paper as shown in the diagram so that the dot is just above the level of water in the jar.
3. The water rises by capillary action and carries the dyes in the ink with it at different speeds. Therefore, the dyes in the ink are separated and different colours can be seen.

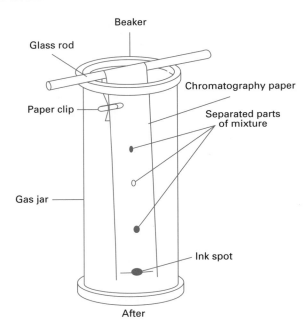

After

Use of Chromatography

Chromatography is used to test urine samples from athletes for drugs and to test food samples for hormones.

Solutions

A **solution** is a mixture of a solute and a solvent, e.g. sugar and water.
The liquid is called the **solvent**, e.g. water.
The substance that dissolves in the liquid is called the **solute**, e.g. sugar.

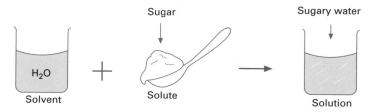

- **Dilute solution:** Where a small amount of solute is dissolved in a large amount of solvent, e.g. a little salt in a large volume of water.
- **Concentrated solution:** Where a large amount of solute is dissolved in a small volume of solvent, e.g. a lot of salt is dissolved in a small volume of water.
- **Saturated solution:** Contains as much solute as can be dissolved at a given temperature. If the temperature is raised, the volume of the liquid increases and more solute can be dissolved.
- **Crystallisation:** If a hot saturated solution is allowed to cool slowly, the solute will come out of the solution as crystals.

Mandatory experiment: Grow copper sulphate crystals.

1. Add some copper sulphate crystals to a cool saturated solution of copper sulphate in a test tube. They do not dissolve.
2. Heat the test tube over a Bunsen burner until the crystals dissolve.
3. Pour the hot concentrated solution of copper sulphate into a beaker to cool, as shown in the diagram.

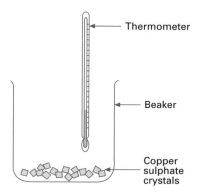

Result: After a few hours, blue crystals of copper sulphate will be seen. It is important to note that copper sulphate is poisonous and can be used in weed killers, so the crystals should not be handled.

The solubility of a substance is the maximum amount of a substance that can be dissolved in 100 g of solvent at a particular temperature. For example, the solubility of a substance in water is the mass of the substance that will dissolve in 100 cm^3 (100 g) of water at a particular temperature.

Experiment: Investigate the solubility of a substance at different temperatures.

1. Measure 100 cm^3 of water into a beaker using a graduated cylinder. Find the mass of the beaker and water using a balance.
2. Note the temperature of the water with the thermometer.
3. Add some copper sulphate to the water and stir well to dissolve.
4. Keep adding the copper sulphate to the water until no more will dissolve at that temperature.
5. Reweigh the beaker and contents. Subtract the mass of the beaker and water from this reading to find the mass of copper sulphate used.
6. Repeat steps 1 to 5 for higher temperatures.

Conclusion: It will be noted that more solid will dissolve at a higher temperature. Therefore, solubility increases as temperature increases.

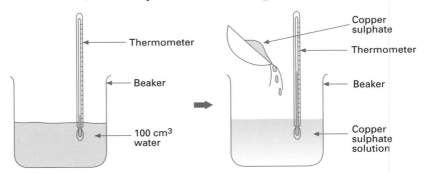

Drawing a Solubility Curve for Copper Sulphate in Water

The following results were obtained in the previous experiment:

Temperature (°C)	0	10	20	30	40	50	60
Solubility (mass of copper sulphate)	15	18	20	25	30	34	40

From the table, we can draw a solubility curve for copper sulphate in water at different temperatures.

Conclusion from curve: It can be seen from the curve that a greater mass of copper sulphate dissolves at higher temperatures. Therefore, solubility increases as the temperature increases.

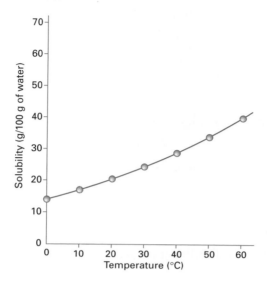

Chapter 18
Air, Oxygen and Carbon Dioxide

Air is a mixture of gases.

- The gases in air are physically combined and can be separated.
- The percentage of these gases can vary.

The following table shows the percentage of gases in air.

Gas in air	Percentage
Nitrogen	78%
Oxygen	21%
Carbon dioxide	0.03%
Noble gas argon	approx 1%
Water vapour	varies

Mandatory experiment: Show that the air contains 21 per cent oxygen.

1. Set up the apparatus as shown in the diagram.

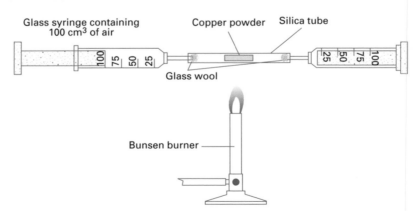

2. Fill one glass syringe with 100 cm³ of air. The other syringe should have no air at the start.

3. Heat the copper strongly.

4. Push the air from the left syringe over the copper to the right syringe. The copper will turn from brown to grey-black as it is reacting with oxygen in the air to form copper oxide.

5. Push the air forwards and backwards from one syringe to the other so that all the oxygen in the air reacts.

6. Allow to cool when the volume of air remains steady.

7. Push all the air into the left syringe and measure the new volume.

Results and conclusion:

*   Volume of air before heating = 100 cm^3
*   Volume of air after heating = 79 cm^3
*   Volume of oxygen present in 100 cm^3 = 21 cm^3

Conclusion: The percentage of oxygen in the air = $\dfrac{21}{100}$ = 21%.

Mandatory experiment: Show that there is water vapour in the air.

1. Place a mixture of ice and salt into a test tube and place a stopper in the tube.

2. Place the tube in a clamp, as shown in the diagram. Leave for 30 minutes.

3. It will be noticed that drops of water are formed on the outside of the tube.

4. To prove that this is water, place some blue cobalt chloride in the film of water.

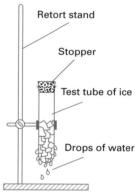

Conclusion: The cobalt chloride turns pink, proving that water present in the air has condensed on the cold test tube.

Mandatory experiment: Show there is carbon dioxide present in the air.

1. Set up the apparatus as shown in the diagram.

2. Using a vacuum pump, draw a current of air through the lime water in the jar.

3. After a few minutes, the lime water turns milky.

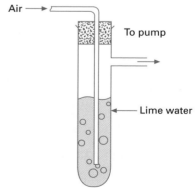

Conclusion: Air contains carbon dioxide.

Preparation of Oxygen Gas

Oxygen is prepared by the chemical breakdown of hydrogen peroxide using manganese dioxide as a catalyst.

Word equation:

$$\text{hydrogen peroxide} \xrightarrow{\text{manganese dioxide}} \text{oxygen} + \text{water}$$

Chemical equation:

$$H_2O_2 \xrightarrow{MnO_2} O_2 + H_2O$$

Mandatory experiment: Prepare and collect oxygen gas.

1. Set up the apparatus as shown in the diagram.
2. Open the tap in the tap funnel and add the hydrogen peroxide slowly to the black solid manganese dioxide.
3. The gas is collected over water, as shown, as it is only slightly soluble in water.
4. Collect three gas jars of the gas for tests.

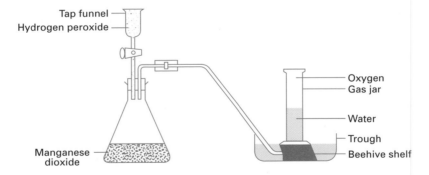

Properties of Oxygen

Physical properties	Chemical properties
Colourless, odourless, tasteless	Supports combustion, i.e. helps things to burn
Slightly heavier than air	Does not burn itself
Slightly soluble in water	Neutral gas. Neither an acid nor a base. No effect on litmus

Oxygen

Uses of oxygen:

- Burning, e.g. used in welding.
- Breathing.

If a glowing splint is placed in a gas jar of oxygen, it will relight, showing that oxygen supports combustion.

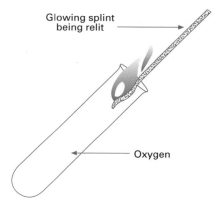

Metals and non-metals burn in oxygen, forming oxides.

Experiment: Burning the metal magnesium in oxygen.

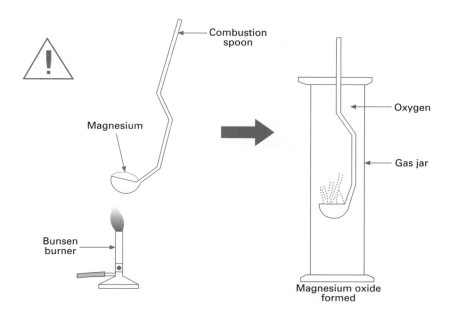

1. Heat a piece of magnesium ribbon in a combustion spoon.
2. Place the spoon in a gas jar of oxygen, as shown. The magnesium burns with a bright flash.
3. Magnesium oxide (a white powder) is formed. When this is tested with moist red litmus, it turns blue.

Conclusion: Magnesium oxide is basic.

Experiment: Burning the non-metal carbon in oxygen.
1. Heat a small amount of charcoal on a combustion spoon and burn in a gas jar of oxygen.
2. The charcoal, which is mainly carbon, burns with a yellow flame, producing carbon dioxide.
3. Add some water to the jar and shake well.
4. Test the solution with blue litmus and it turns red.
5. Test the solution with lime water and it turns milky.

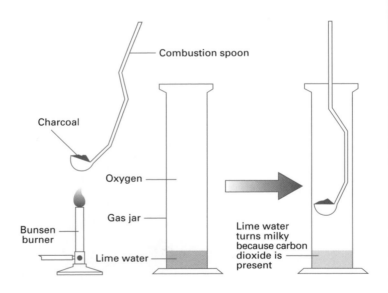

Conclusion: Burning carbon in oxygen produces carbon dioxide, which is an acid gas.

General conclusion: The oxides of metals, e.g. magnesium oxide, are basic. The oxides of non-metals, e.g. carbon dioxide, are acidic.

Preparation and Properties of Carbon Dioxide

Carbon dioxide is prepared by the action of dilute hydrochloric acid on calcium carbonate (marble chips).

Word equation:

calcium carbonate+hydrochloric acid=calcium chloride+water+carbon dioxide

Chemical equation:

$$CaCO_3 + 2\ HCl = CaCl_2 + H_2O + CO_2$$

Mandatory experiment: Prepare and collect carbon dioxide gas.
1. Set up the apparatus as shown in the diagram.
2. Add dilute hydrochloric acid slowly to the calcium carbonate.
3. Collect three gas jars of the gas for tests.

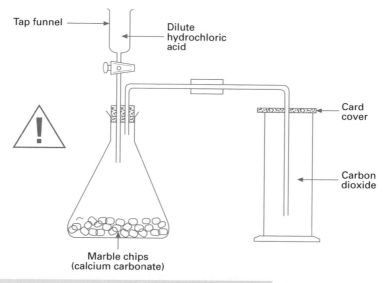

Properties of Carbon Dioxide

Physical properties	Chemical properties
Colourless, odourless, tasteless	Does not support combustion
Slightly soluble in water	Acid gas – turns blue litmus red
Heavier than air	Turns lime water milky

Uses of the Gas

- Used in fire extinguishers as it does not support combustion.
- Used in fizzy drinks.
- Used by plants in photosynthesis to make food.

Experiment: Demonstrate the properties of carbon dioxide.

1. Test for carbon dioxide: it turns lime water milky.

    Limewater is a dilute solution of calcium hydroxide ($Ca(OH)_2$) which reacts with carbon dioxide to form the white solid calcium carbonate. Therefore, if the delivery tube carrying carbon dioxide from the above experiment is placed in a test tube of lime water, it will turn milky.

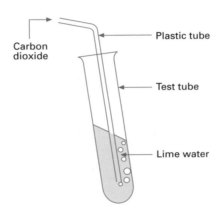

Word equation:

> carbon dioxide + calcium hydroxide = calcium carbonate + water

Chemical equation:

> $CO_2 + Ca(OH)_2 = CaCO_3 + H_2O$

To show that carbon dioxide does not support combustion, put a lighting taper into a gas jar of carbon dioxide – it will be quenched.

To show that carbon dioxide is heavier than air, place a small candle into a gas jar. 'Pour' carbon dioxide from another gas jar into the jar with the candle, as shown in the diagram. The candle will be quenched.

Conclusion: As carbon dioxide is heavier than air, it can be poured from one jar into another.

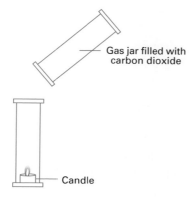

Gas jar filled with carbon dioxide

Candle

To show carbon dioxide is an acid gas, place a piece of wet blue litmus paper in a gas jar of carbon dioxide. It turns red, proving carbon dioxide is an acid.

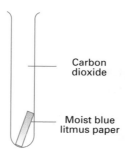

Carbon dioxide

Moist blue litmus paper

Chapter **19**
Water and Hardness of Water

Properties of Water

- Water is a compound of the elements hydrogen and oxygen.
- Its boiling point is 100°C and its freezing point is 0°C.
- Water is a very good solvent. However, certain substances will not dissolve in it, e.g. iodine, oil, chewing gum or nail varnish. Turpentine will dissolve oil and acetone will dissolve nail varnish.
- Test for water: it turns blue cobalt chloride paper pink.

Water Cycle

Our supply of water never runs out because it is regenerated by the **water cycle**. There are five stages in the water cycle:

1. Evaporation: Heat from the sun causes water to evaporate from the oceans.
2. Condensation: The water vapour cools to form clouds.
3. Precipitation: The water vapour cools and falls as rain.
4. The rainwater soaks into the ground and seeps into rivers and streams.
5. The rivers and streams carry the water back to the oceans.

Water Treatment for Domestic Use

There are various stages that water goes through before it is deemed fit for human use.

1. **Screening:** The water is passed through metal screens to remove large pieces of dirt and vegetation.

2. **Settling:** The water is then stored in large settling tanks or reservoirs, which allows the clay particles to settle out at the bottom.

3. **Filtration:** The water is passed through filter beds with fine sand on top and coarse sand and pebbles below. Very small particles of dirt are removed this way.

4. **Chlorination:** Small amounts of chlorine are added to the water to kill bacteria.

5. **Fluoridation:** Small amounts of fluoride are added to the water to build up the enamel on teeth and prevent tooth decay.

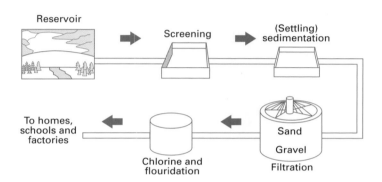

Hard and Soft Water

Hard water is water that does not form a lather with soap but forms a scum instead. Soft water lathers easily with soap.

The presence of calcium and magnesium ions in the water cause hardness. There are two types of hardness: temporary and permanent.

Temporary hardness is caused by the presence of calcium hydrogen carbonate in the water. It is found in limestone areas where the carbonic acid in rain water reacts with the calcium carbonate, producing calcium hydrogen carbonate, which dissolves in the water, causing hardness.

Temporary hardness can be removed by boiling the water, but permanent hardness cannot.

Permanent hardness is caused by calcium chloride and calcium sulphate. It can also be caused by magnesium chloride and magnesium sulphate. Permanent hardness can be removed by ion exchange.

Removal of Permanent Hardness by Ion Exchange

This process involves swapping ions that don't cause hardness with the calcium and magnesium ions that do cause hardness. The basic idea is that hard water containing calcium ions is passed through a resin, as shown in the diagram.

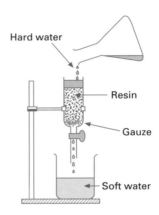

The positive ions in the water, e.g. calcium ions (Ca^{++}), are swapped with hydrogen ions (H^+), and the negative ions are swapped with hydroxide ions (OH^-). Then the H^+ ions and the OH^- ions combine to form water. The water is now soft and is called deionised water.

Advantages of hard water:

- Contains calcium, which is good for bones and teeth.
- Tastes better.
- Good for brewing.

Disadvantages of hard water:

- Wastes soap.
- It produces lime scale, which can block heating pipes.

Mandatory experiment: Test for hardness in a number of water samples.
In this experiment, three samples of water are examined:

Sample A = distilled water
Sample B = hard water from a limestone area
Sample C = boiled sample of hard water from a limestone area

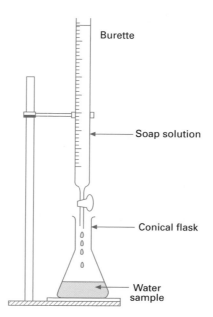

Burette

Soap solution

Conical flask

Water sample

1. Place some soap solution in a burette.

2. Place 25 cm³ of sample A (distilled water) in a conical flask. Add 2 cm³ of soap solution. Shake the flask. A permanent lather of soap is formed. This proves there is no hardness present.

3. Place 25 cm³ of sample B (hard water) in a conical flask. Add 2 cm³ of soap solution. Shake the flask. A permanent lather is not formed. In fact, it takes 20 cm³ of soap solution to produce a lather, proving that the water is hard.

4. Place 25 cm³ of sample C (boiled hard water) in a conical flask. Add 2 cm³ of soap solution. Keep adding soap solution until a permanent lather is formed. Less soap will be required as in the case of the B sample, as boiling removes the temporary hardness.

Mandatory experiment: Show that water contains dissolved solids.

1. Take a sample of water from a river or pond.

2. Filter the sample using filter paper to remove suspended matter such as clay particles.

3. Place a small volume, e.g. 50 cm³, of the filtered water in an evaporating dish.

4. Place the dish on a water bath, as shown, and evaporate the water.

5. When all the water has evaporated, remove the dish and allow to cool.

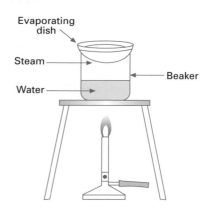

Evaporating dish

Steam

Water

Beaker

Conclusion: A small amount of solid will be seen at the bottom of the dish, proving the presence of dissolved solids in water. The experiment can be repeated for other samples. Different samples of water contain different amounts of dissolved solids.

Mandatory Experiment: Obtain a sample of pure water from sea water.
To separate pure water from sea water, a distillation apparatus is used, as in the separation of alcohol and water.

1. Set up the distillation apparatus.
2. Place the sea water in the flask. Heat to 100°C, the boiling point of water. The water vapour is cooled back to water in the condenser and the water is collected, as shown in the conical flask. The salt remains in the flask.

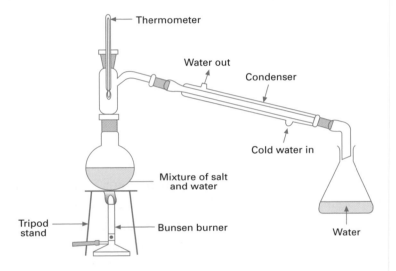

Electrolysis and the Electrolysis of Water

Electrolysis is a chemical change brought about by an electric current.
An **electrolyte** is a solution that can conduct an electric current, e.g. a solution that contains ions, such as hydrochloric acid or sulphuric acid.

Experiment: Show by electrolysis that water is composed of hydrogen and oxygen gases.
In this experiment, the electrolyte is a dilute solution of sulphuric acid. This solution is placed in a Hoffman voltameter, as shown in the diagram.

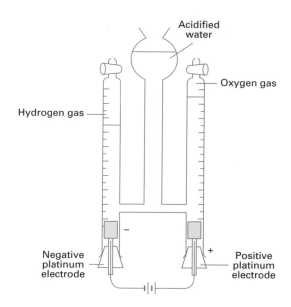

1. Switch on the current. Hydrogen gas collects at the negative electrode, or cathode. Note that both electrodes are made of platinum or carbon.

2. Oxygen gas collects at the positive electrode, or anode. Note that there is twice as much hydrogen gas as oxygen gas. This proves that the formula for water is H_2O.

3. The sulphuric acid provides ions to carry the current.

The current would not flow unless these ions were present. This experiment can also be used to demonstrate the chemical effect of an electric current.

Chapter **20**
The Periodic Table: Metals and Non-metal Groups

In the periodic table, a **period** is a horizontal row of elements and a **group** is a vertical column of elements.

A Russian scientist called Mendeleev arranged the elements into periods and groups. He put elements with similar properties into the same group. In the periodic table below, metals are on the left side of the zig-zag line and non-metals are on the right side.

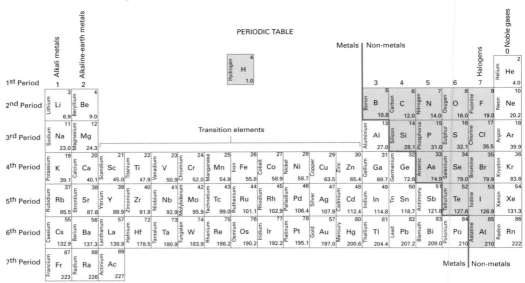

Important Groups in the Periodic Table

All the atoms of elements in a particular group have the same number of electrons in their outer level. For example, Group 1 elements, e.g. sodium, have one electron in their outer level.

Group 1 elements are called the alkali metals. This group includes lithium (Li), sodium (Na) and potassium (K). This group of elements is highly reactive, as their atoms want to lose one electron and are unstable.

Goup 2 elements are called the alkaline earth metals. This group includes beryllium (Be), magnesium (Mg) and calcium (Ca). The atoms of these elements want to lose two electrons. They are reactive, but not as reactive as the alkali metals.

Group 7 elements are called the halogens. These elements are gases, e.g. fluorine (F) and chlorine (Cl). Their atoms want to gain one electron. They are highly reactive, as they are unstable.

Group O elements are called the noble gases. Their atoms have full shells of electrons and don't want to gain or lose electrons. Therefore, they are stable and not reactive, e.g. helium (He), neon (Ne) and argon (Ar). Helium gas is used in balloons, as it is safe and not reactive.

Alkali and Alkaline Earth Metals

Physical properties of alkali (Group 1) metals:
- Soft metals that can be easily cut with a knife.
- Light metals (low density) and float on water.

Chemical properties:
- They are highly reactive, as they want to lose only one electron.
- They react with water vapour and oxygen in the air and therefore must be stored in oil. They cannot be found free in nature.

Reactions of Alkali Metals

(a) With oxygen: Sodium burns rapidly in oxygen with a yellow flame. It forms a white oxide called sodium oxide. It also reacts with oxygen in the air.

Word equation: sodium + oxygen = sodium oxide

Chemical equation: $2\,Na + \frac{1}{2}\,O_2 = Na_2O$

(b) Potassium reacts with oxygen, producing potassium oxide.

Word equation: potassium + oxygen = potassium oxide

Chemical equation: $2K + \frac{1}{2}\,O_2 = K_2O$

(c) Lithium reacts with oxygen to produce lithium oxide.

Word equation: lithium + oxygen = lithium oxide

Chemical equation: $2Li + \frac{1}{2} O_2 = Li_2O$

Oxides of Metals and Non-Metals

Generally, **oxides of metals** are basic and turn red litmus blue. Therefore, if some red litmus solution was added to a gas jar with sodium oxide, it would turn blue. Also note that **oxides of non-metals** are basic, e.g. carbon dioxide gas turns moist blue litmus paper red.

Reactions of Alkali Metals with Water

All alkali metals react vigorously with water, producing hydrogen gas and the metal hydroxide.

(a) Reaction of sodium with water: Extreme care must be taken, as this reaction is very vigorous. Eye goggles should be worn. A small piece of sodium is placed in a water bath covered with a glass lid, as shown in the diagram.

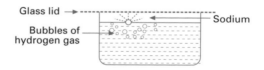

The sodium fizzes around on the top of the water, releasing hydrogen gas. Sparks may be observed due to the violent nature of the reaction, which is:

sodium + water = sodium hydroxide + hydrogen gas

(b) The reaction of potassium with water is more vigorous than in the case of sodium. The word equation for this reaction is:

potassium + water = potassium hydroxide + hydrogen gas

(c) Reaction of lithium with water:

lithium + water = lithium hydroxide + hydrogen gas

Note that this reaction is less vigorous than in the cases of sodium or potassium.

Reactivity increases as we go down the group of metals in Group 1. Therefore, potassium is more reactive than sodium, sodium is more reactive than lithium, and so on.

The reason that potassium is the most reactive is that potassium is a bigger atom than the other two atoms and its outer electron is further away from the positive nucleus and therefore is less tightly held, as the attraction is not as strong. This makes potassium more reactive, as it can lose its electron more easily.

Alkaline Earth Metals (Group 2)

Examples of **alkaline earth metals (Group 2)** metals are magnesium (Mg) and calcium (Ca). The atoms of these elements want to lose two electrons. They are not as reactive as the alkali metals. Unlike the alkali metals, the alkaline earth metals don't have to be stored in oil, as they are not as reactive with oxygen or water vapour in the air.

Reaction with water:
- Magnesium will only react very slowly with cold water, but it will react with steam as:

  magnesium + water (steam) = magnesium oxide + hydrogen gas
- Calcium reacts vigorously with cold water, as follows:

  calcium + water (cold) = calcium hydroxide and hydrogen gas

Reaction with oxygen:
- If magnesium is burned in air, it forms magnesium oxide:

  magnesium + oxygen = magnesium oxide
- Calcium reacts more vigorously with oxygen, producing calcium oxide:

  calcium + oxygen = calcium oxide

As in the case of the alkali metals, the reactivity increases as you go down Group 2, as calcium is more reactive than magnesium.

Chapter **21**
Metals, Metal Alloys and Reactivity of Metals

Properties of Metals

- They are malleable, i.e. can be hammered into flat sheets, e.g. lead.
- They are ductile, i.e. can be stretched out into thin wires, e.g. copper wires for electric wiring.
- They are good conductors of heat and electricity.
- They have high melting and boiling points.
- They have a shiny (lustrous) appearance when polished.

Corrosion of Metals

Corrosion is where a metal reacts with oxygen in the air to form an oxide. It is an example of a chemical reaction where oxidation takes place.

Example: Iron combines with oxygen in the air in the presence of water to form iron oxide or rust. Rusting, then, is a particular example of corrosion. In corrosion, metals return to the form of an ore.

Mandatory experiment: Investigate the conditions needed for rusting. There are two conditions needed for rusting: water and oxygen.

1. Set up the apparatus as shown in the diagram.

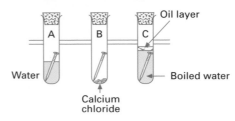

2. Leave the test tubes as shown for one week and then check each for signs of rusting. To ensure a fair test, the iron nails used should be identical.
3. The iron nail in test tube A shows signs of rusting, as it had both water and oxygen.
4. The nail in test tube B shows no rust, as it had no water. Calcium chloride is a drying agent and removes water form the air.
5. The nail in test tube C does not rust, as there is no oxygen. Boiling the water removes oxygen from it and the oil layer prevents any oxygen returning to the water from the air

Conclusion: Water and oxygen are needed for rusting to occur.

Methods of preventing corrosion or rusting:
- Painting.
- Greasing and oiling.
- Galvanising, e.g. coating iron with a layer of zinc.
- Chromium plating, e.g. coating steel with a layer of chromium. This is used in car bumpers, for example.

Alloys

An **alloy** is a mixture of metals or a mixture of a metal and a solid.

Examples of alloys and their uses:
- Steel is a mixture of carbon and iron. Steel is much harder than iron and is used in machinery and ships.
- Brass is a mixture of copper and zinc. It is used in door handles and ornaments.
- Bronze is a mixture of copper and tin. It is used in statues and ornaments.
- Solder is mixture of lead and tin. It has a low melting point and is used in joining electrical wires.

Activity Series of Metals

The **activity series of metals** is a list of metals based on how reactive they are. The most reactive metals are placed at the top of the series and the least reactive at the bottom. As we have already noted, the Group 1 metals are the most reactive, closely followed by the not quite as reactive Group 2 metals. Activity series of metals (use this phrase to help you remember):

1. Potassium (K)	poor	Most reactive
2. Sodium (Na)	sod	
3. Calcium (Ca)	can't	
4. Magnesium (Mg)	make	
5. Aluminium (Al)	a	
6. Zinc (Zn)	zero	
7. Iron (Fe)	in	
8. Lead (Pb)	leaving	
9. Hydrogen (H)*	higher	
10. Copper (Cu)	chemistry	
11. Silver (Ag)	silly	
12. Gold (Au)	goose	Least reactive

*Note that hydrogen is a gas, not a metal, but is placed here for comparison purposes. Also note that any metal below hydrogen will not react with acids, e.g. copper.

Comparison of Reactions of Four Metals from the Activity Series

For the Junior Cert, the reactions of calcium, magnesium, zinc and copper with water and acid must be examined.
What is the decreasing order of reactivity of the four metals calcium, magnesium, zinc and copper? Using the above table, the order of decreasing reactivity is: calcium, magnesium, zinc, copper.

Experiment: Compare the reactions of calcium, magnesium, zinc and copper with water and dilute acid.
In the following experiments to test the reactions of metals with water and acid, the student can carry out a fair test by ensuring that:
• The pieces of metal are approximately the same size.
• The temperature of acid and water are the same.
• The concentration of the acid is the same.

(A) Reaction with water

1. Set up the apparatus as shown in the diagram.

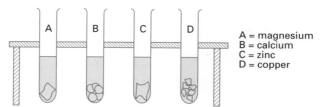

2. For a fair test to occur, place an equal amount of water in each test tube and ensure that the pieces of metal are the same size and that the temperature of the water is the same.
3. Place a sample of magnesium, calcium, zinc and copper into each test tube.

Results and conclusion: Only calcium reacts with cold water, thus it is the most reactive metal. Magnesium takes several days to react with cold water but will react with steam. Zinc will only react with steam and copper does not react with water.

(B) Reaction with dilute hydrochloric acid

1. Repeat steps 1, 2 and 3 of the previous experiment, but this time use dilute hydrochloric acid instead of water.
2. Ensure that the concentration and temperature of acid is the same for the four metals. Extreme care must be taken with calcium for this test, as it is very reactive.

Results: Calcium is more reactive than magnesium or zinc. There is no reaction with copper.

Conclusion: The order of increasing reactivity follows the activity series: calcium is the most reactive and copper is the least reactive. The following table summarises the reactions:

Metal	Reaction with water	Reaction with dilute HCl
Calcium	Most reactive. Reacts with cold water	Most reactive, releasing hydrogen gas
Magnesium	Only reacts with steam	Quite vigorous, releasing hydrogen gas
Zinc	Reacts slowly with steam	Less vigorous reaction than with magnesium. Hydrogen gas is released
Copper	No reaction	No reaction

Mandatory experiment: React zinc with hydrochloric acid.

Zinc metal reacts with hydrochloric acid, producing zinc chloride and hydrogen gas. The word equation for the reaction is:

$$\boxed{\text{zinc + hydrochloric acid = zinc chloride + hydrogen}}$$

The chemical equation for the reaction is:

$$\boxed{Zn + 2HCl = ZnCl_2 + H_2}$$

1. Set up the apparatus as shown in the diagram.

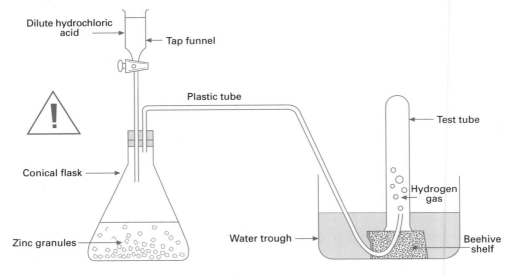

2. Using the tap funnel, add dilute hydrochloric acid to the zinc.

3. Collect five test tubes of the gas.

4. Stopper the test tubes, as hydrogen is much lighter than air.

5. Test for hydrogen by inserting a lighting splint into a test tube of the gas. A popping sound is heard. This proves that the gas is hydrogen, as hydrogen forms an explosive mixture with air.

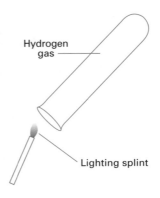

Chapter 22
Structure of the Atom

An **atom** is the smallest part of an element that can take part in a chemical reaction. Atoms are extremely small – about 1 billion atoms are needed to make a full stop at the end of a sentence.

There are three main types of particle in the atom: **protons, neutrons** and **electrons**. The protons and neutrons are located in the central part of the atom, called the nucleus. The electrons have a negative charge and spin around the nucleus, as they are attracted to the positive charge of the protons in the nucleus. The electrons are arranged in orbits, or shells, with two electrons in the first shell, eight electrons in the second shell, and so on.

Properties of Protons, Neutrons and Electrons

Particle	Mass	Charge	Location
Proton	1 amu (atomic mass unit)	+1	Nucleus
Electron	$\frac{1}{1840}$ amu	−1	Orbits nucleus
Neutron	1 amu	No charge	Nucleus

Structures of Atoms

Hydrogen

In the periodic table, each atom is given two numbers. In the case of hydrogen, the numbers are as follows:

1   The top number is called the atomic number.

H

1.008 = 1 The bottom number (to the nearest whole number) is called the mass number.

The **atomic number** is the number of protons in an atom, e.g. one proton in hydrogen.

In a neutral atom, the number of protons is equal to the number of electrons, therefore hydrogen has one electron.

The **mass number** is the number of protons and neutrons.

The number of neutrons = mass number – atomic number = 1 – 1 = 0 neutrons in the hydrogen atom. The hydrogen atom has one proton, one electron and no neutrons.

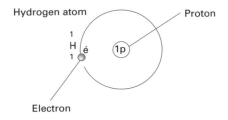

Stable atoms

Helium and neon in Group O (noble gases) are two examples of stable atoms. The helium and neon atoms have the following atomic and mass numbers and structures:

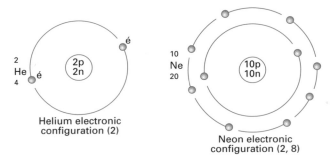

Helium electronic
configuration (2)

Neon electronic
configuration (2, 8)

Helium is very stable, as its first orbit, or shell, is full with two electrons. Neon is also stable, as its first and second levels are full. (The second level fits eight electrons). Both of these atoms are therefore very non-reactive, as they do not want to lose or gain electrons.

Unstable atoms

Sodium in Group 1 (the alkali metals) is an example of an unstable atom. In the periodic table, sodium appears as follows:

11 = atomic number = 11 protons

Na

23 = mass number

Therefore, sodium has eleven protons and twelve neutrons (23 − 11).

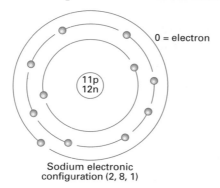

0 = electron

Sodium electronic
configuration (2, 8, 1)

The sodium atom is not stable, as it wants to lose one electron from its outer shell to have a stable structure like neon. Therefore, it is highly reactive with water and oxygen, which explains why it is stored in oil.

Isotopes

Isotopes are atoms of the same element that have different numbers of neutrons. All atoms of the same element are not identical. They can have different mass numbers and therefore have different numbers of neutrons. For example, carbon can exist in two forms – carbon 12 or carbon 14. Their structures are as follows:

Carbon 12 (C_6^{12}) Carbon 14 (C_6^{14})

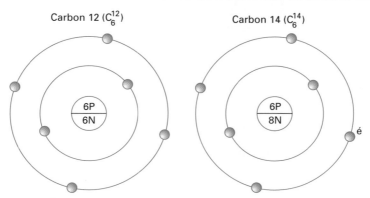

6P
6N

6P
8N

é

The carbon 12 (C^{12}) isotope has six protons and six neutrons, whereas the carbon 14 (C^{14}) isotope has six protons and eight neutrons. Therefore, carbon 14 has two extra neutrons, which makes it a heavier atom.

Carbon 14 is used in carbon dating, i.e. finding the age of archaeological specimens.

Electronic Configuration

Electronic configuration means the way the electrons are arranged into the various shells or orbits.

Neils Bohr put forward the theory that electrons spin around the nucleus in different orbits. The first orbit, or level, fits two electrons, the second orbit fits eight electrons, and so on. Therefore, the sodium atom has eleven electrons, so the electronic configuration of sodium is as follows:

1st orbit	2nd orbit	3rd orbit
2	8	1

Another unstable atom is the chlorine atom in Group 7 (the halogens). In the periodic table, chlorine appears as follows:

17
Cl
35.457 = 35

Therefore, chlorine has seventeen protons, seventeen electrons and eighteen neutrons (35 − 17 = 18). The electronic configuration of chlorine is 2, 8, 7.

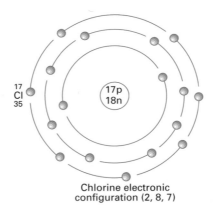

Chlorine electronic
configuration (2, 8, 7)

The chlorine atom is unstable as it wants to gain one electron to have eight electrons in its outer orbit, like the noble gas argon.

The calcium atom in Group 2 (the alkaline earth metals) appears as follows in the periodic table:

20
C$_a$
40

Therefore, the structure of calcium is as shown in the diagram.

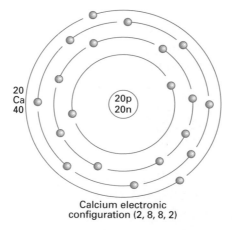

Calcium electronic
configuration (2, 8, 8, 2)

The calcium atom wants to lose two electrons to have a stable structure like argon (2, 8, 8). The electronic configuration of calcium is 2, 8, 8, 2.

Chapter **23**
Ionic and Covalent Bonding

Bonding occurs when atoms of one element combine with atoms of the same element or with another element.

There are two main types of bonding: ionic and covalent.

Ions and Ionic Bonding

An **ion** is formed when an atom loses or gains one or more electrons. A positive ion is formed when an atom loses electrons. For example, when the sodium atom (Na) loses an electron, it becomes the sodium ion (Na^+).

A negative ion is formed when an atom gains electrons. For example, when the chlorine atom gains electrons, it becomes the chloride ion (Cl^-).

Ionic bonding is where there is a transfer of electrons between atoms. The force of attraction between positive and negative ions holds the bond together, e.g. the attraction between Na^+ and Cl^- ions forms an ionic bond.

Octet rule: Most atoms want to have eight electrons in their outer level, like the noble gases, as this is a stable structure. This explains why the noble gases such as neon and argon are very stable and do not react. Neon gas is used in neon lights, as it is not reactive.

Ionic Bonding in Sodium Chloride

The sodium atom is not stable. It has one electron in its outer level and wants to lose it to have a stable structure like neon. The chlorine atom is not stable either, as it needs one electron to fill its outer level. Therefore, the sodium atom gives its outer electron to chlorine, as shown in Figure 1.

The sodium atom becomes the positive sodium ion (Na^+), as it has lost an electron, and the chlorine atom becomes a negative chloride ion (Cl^-), as it has gained an electron.

Experiment: Compare the ability of ionic and covalent compounds to conduct electricity.

Ionic compounds, e.g. sodium chloride (NaCl), consist of positive and negative ions that can conduct an electric current when free to move in a solution. Covalent compounds, e.g. paraffin oil, have no ions and therefore do not conduct a current. The following experiment will show this.

1. Set up the circuit as shown in the diagram.

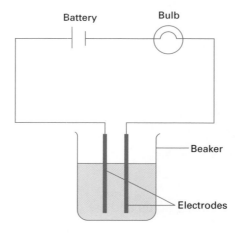

2. Put a covalent liquid into the beaker, e.g. distilled water (pure water does not carry a current) or paraffin oil.

3. The bulb will not light when the current is switched on.

4. Now place a solution of an ionic substance, e.g. sodium chloride, in the beaker. Switch on the current. This time the bulb lights, proving that ionic substances conduct electricity and covalent substances do not.

Chapter **24**
Acids and Bases

Acids and **bases** are two important groups of chemicals.

Acids

Examples of acids used in the school lab are:

- Hydrochloric acid (HCl).
- Sulphuric acid (H_2SO_4).
- Nitric acid (HNO_3).

The above three acids are strong acids and are dangerous, as they can burn skin, clothing, etc.

Everyday acids used in the home are:

- Vinegar (ethanoic acid).
- Citric acid in oranges and lemons.
- Lactic acid in sour milk.
- Carbonic acid in soft drinks, e.g. 7-Up.

The above acids are weak and are not dangerous and can be consumed by the body.

Properties of acids in general:

- Sharp taste.
- Turns blue litmus red.
- Can be corrosive, i.e. strong acids like hydrochloric acid attack skin, metal, etc.
- Most acids react with metals, forming salts and releasing hydrogen gas.
- Acids react with bases to form salts and water.

Bases

A base that dissolves in water is an alkali.

Examples of bases used in the school lab are:

- Sodium hydroxide (NaOH).
- Calcium hydroxide $Ca(OH)_2$ or any metal hydroxide.
- Ammonia (NH_3).
- Calcium carbonate ($CaCO_3$).

Everyday bases used in the home are:

- Toothpaste.
- Soap.
- Oven cleaner.
- Bread soda.

Properties of bases in general:

- Soapy feel.
- Turns red litmus blue.
- Can be corrosive, i.e. strong bases like sodium hydroxide are corrosive and are used to clear drains.

Indicators

An **indicator** is a substance that can show if a solution is an acid or a base by a colour change, e.g. litmus.

- Acids turn blue litmus red.
- Bases turn red litmus blue.
- To remember: RABB = red in acid, blue in base.

The pH Scale

The **pH scale** measures how acidic or basic a solution is.

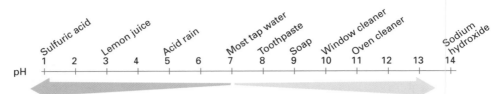

The smaller the number, the stronger the acid   The larger the number, the stronger the alkali

On the pH scale:

- Acids are between 0 and 7.

- Neutral substances (neither acidic nor basic), e.g. water, are equal to 7.

- Bases are between 7 and 14.

The stronger the acid, the lower its pH, e.g. hydrochloric acid has a pH of 1. The stronger the base, the higher the pH, e.g. sodium hydroxide has a pH of 14.

Use of Universal Indicator to Find Exact pH

Universal indicator can come in the form of a solution or paper. It has a range of colours. Each colour gives a pH value.

Note that accurate values of pH can also be measured using a pH meter.

Experiment: Find the pH of a variety of chemicals using universal indicator.

1. Place five clean, dry test tubes in a test tube rack.

2. Add about 10 cm^3 of different solutions to each tube: A = hydrochloric acid, B = lemon juice, C = rain water, D = soap, E = sodium hydroxide.

3. Now add some universal indicator (paper or solution) to each test tube and compare the colour obtained with the colour chart to find the pH of the solution.

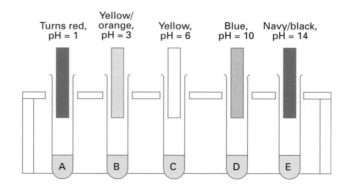

Results and conclusions:

Solution	Colour	pH (acid or base)
A = dilute HCl	Red	1 (strong acid)
B = lemon juice	Orange	3 (weak acid)
C = rain water	Yellow	6 (slightly acid)
D = soap	Blue	10 (weak base)
E = sodium hydroxide	Violet (dark blue)	14 (strong base)

Neutralisation of Acids and Bases

Neutralisation occurs when an acid reacts with a base and forms a salt and water.

Example: When hydrochloric acid reacts with sodium hydroxide, the following products are formed:

Word equation:

hydrochloric acid + sodium hydroxide → sodium chloride + water

Chemical equation: $HCl + NaOH \rightarrow NaCl + H_2O$

Mandatory experiment: Prepare a salt by neutralising an acid with a base in a titration.

1. Set up the apparatus as shown in the diagram.

2. The burette is filled with hydrochloric acid. 20 cm³ of sodium hydroxide is added to the conical flask using a pipette.

3. A few drops of litmus indicator are added to the conical flask and the base turns blue.

4. Add the acid slowly from the burette until the indicator changes from blue to pink. Note

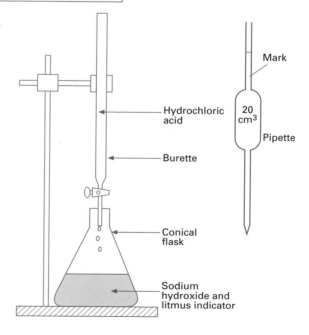

Mark

Hydrochloric acid

20 cm³

Pipette

Burette

Conical flask

Sodium hydroxide and litmus indicator

the volume of acid needed. This is called the end point and the whole process is called a titration. Let's say that the volume at the end point is 20 cm^3.

5. In a separate beaker, add the same volumes of acid and base together, i.e. 20 cm^3 of each, but this time use no indicator.

6. The HCl acid and NaOH base will neutralise in the beaker, forming the salt sodium chloride and water.

7. Now place the beaker in an oven set at 100°C (boiling point of water). The water will evaporate, leaving the salt sodium chloride behind.

Chapter 25
Chemistry in Everyday Life

Fossil Fuels

Fossil fuels, e.g. coal, oil, peat, are formed from the decay of plants and animals over millions of years. They are non-renewable, i.e. can only be used once. Renewable fuels such as wind, waves and biomass (renewable energy made from plant material, e.g. ethanol made from sugar) can be used again and again. Natural gas is a fossil fuel and contains mainly methane (CH_4). This gas burns cleanly with no smoke or fumes. When a fossil fuel like methane is burned in oxygen, it produces carbon dioxide and water vapour, as shown by the following equation.

$$\underset{\text{methane}}{CH_4} + 2\,O_2 = \underset{\text{carbon dioxide}}{CO_2} + \underset{\text{water}}{2\,H_2O}$$

The three conditions needed for burning are heat, fuel and oxygen.
Common fire extinguishers are carbon dioxide and dry powder extinguishers. These extinguishers work by excluding oxygen from the fire.

Acid Rain

Acid rain is rain water with a pH less than 5.5. Normal rain water is slightly acidic (pH 5.5) because it dissolves carbon dioxide as it passes through the atmosphere to form carbonic acid, as shown by the following equation.

$$\underset{\text{carbon dioxide}}{CO_2} + \underset{\text{water}}{H_2O} = \underset{\text{carbonic acid}}{H_2CO_3}$$

What causes acid rain? Sulphur dioxide and oxides of nitrogen.
In areas where there is a lot of industry, the burning of fossil fuels releases sulphur dioxide (SO_2) and oxides of nitrogen, e.g. NO_2, into the atmosphere. Sulphur dioxide contributes to acid rain, as it dissolves in rain water to form sulphurous acid, as shown by the following equation.

$$\boxed{\begin{array}{ccc} SO_2 & + H_2O = & H_2SO_3 \\ \text{sulphur dioxide} & \text{water} & \text{sulphurous acid} \end{array}}$$

Sulphurous acid then reacts with oxygen in the air to form sulphuric acid. In a similar way, oxides of nitrogen form nitric acid. Therefore, the oxides of sulphur and nitrogen make the rain water more acidic (less than 5.5) and it is called acid rain.

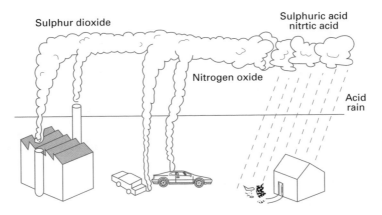

Disadvantages of acid rain:

- Causes fish kills.
- Corrodes limestone buildings.
- Damages roots of trees.

Greenhouse Effect

Our atmosphere behaves like a giant greenhouse in that greenhouse gases allow heat from the sun to pass through them, but they absorb heat that is radiated from the earth and prevent it from escaping.

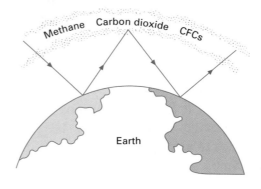

The reason for this is that the incoming heat energy from the sun consists of short wavelengths of ultraviolet (UV) light, which can get through, but the outward heat energy from the earth is long-wavelength infrared light, which cannot penetrate these gases and therefore cannot escape.

The main greenhouse gases are:

- Carbon dioxide.
- Methane.
- CFCs (chlorofluorocarbons from aerosols).

Increases in levels of carbon dioxide and methane in the atmosphere are causing the earth to heat up, i.e. global warming. Increases in the levels of carbon dioxide are due to the burning of fossil fuels. Increases of levels in methane are due to emissions from cattle (and humans!), rubbish dumps, swamps, etc.

Effects of Global Warming

In time, global warming will lead to rises in sea levels and flooding due to melting of polar ice caps.

How to prevent global warming:

- Burn less fossil fuels and use alternative fuels, such as wind and solar.
- Do not use aerosols, which release CFCs into the atmosphere.

Ozone Layer

Ozone (O_3) is formed in the atmosphere when oxygen molecules react with an oxygen atom: $O_2 + \frac{1}{2} O_2 = O_3$ (ozone).

There is a layer of ozone about 25–50 km above the earth's surface that protects people on earth from the harmful effects of the UV radiation from the sun, which can cause skin cancer. This layer is being damaged by the release of CFCs from aerosol cans and fridges. As a result, CFCs are being phased out in many countries.

Plastics

Plastics are manmade materials made from chemicals that are produced from crude oil. The plastic is made by joining together many small molecules, called monomers, to form a large molecule, called a polymer.

The polymer is used to make the plastic, i.e. many small molecules of ethene are joined together to form the polymer polyethene, as shown in the diagram. (Polyethene is commonly known as the plastic polythene.)

Ethene
Monomer ethene

Poly(ethene)
Polymer polythene

General properties of plastics:

- Lightweight.
- Hardwearing.
- Waterproof.
- Easy to clean.
- Can be made very strong.
- Easily moulded into different shapes.
- Cheap to produce.
- Good insulators.

Examples of some plastics and their uses:

Plastic	Properties	Uses
Polythene	Waterproof and easily moulded	Plastic bags and bottles
Nylon	Strong and hardwearing	Clothing and ropes
PVC	Strong and durable	Windows and gutters
Polystyrene	Strong, good insulator	Yoghurt and coffee cups
Perspex	Clear, tough plastic	Plastic lenses for cars

Negative effects of plastics to the environment:

- Plastics are non-biodegradable, which means they cannot be broken down by bacteria and fungi in the environment. Therefore, they don't rot like biodegradable materials such as paper and wood. As a result, plastics can build up in the environment and cause litter problems. To prevent this, most countries now recycle plastics. In Ireland, for example, the government put a levy on plastic bags to limit their use and protect the environment.
- Plastics are also a fire risk. They burn very easily and emit poisonous fumes.

BIOLOGY

Chapter 26
Plant and Animal Cells

Biology is the study of living things or organisms. Living things are divided into two main groups: **plants** and **animals**.

There are seven characteristics of living things:

- **Movement:** Both plants and animals move. Animals have better movement than plants. An example of plant movement is petals opening and closing.

- **Respiration:** Both plants and animals respire where they convert food into energy. The reaction for respiration is:

  glucose + oxygen = energy + carbon dioxide + water

- **Sensitivity:** The ability of a plant or animal to react to changes in its surroundings (environment). Plants are less sensitive than animals and respond to light and water, for example.

- **Feeding:** Green plants can make their own food, but animals cannot. Animals get their food by eating plants and other animals. Green plants make their food by photosynthesis. The reaction for photosynthesis is:

  sunlight + carbon dioxide + water $\xrightarrow{\text{chlorophyll}}$ glucose + oxygen

- **Excretion:** The removal of waste matter from the chemical reactions that go on in the body, e.g. plants and animals release carbon dioxide and water vapour.

- **Reproduction:** Both plants and animals must reproduce or they will become extinct.

- **Growth.**

Cells, Tissues, Organs and Systems

The smallest living unit of a plant or animal is called a cell.

A **tissue** is a group of cells carrying out a certain function, e.g. muscle cells for movement, skin cells for protection.

An **organ** is a group of tissues working together for a certain function, e.g. the heart has muscle and blood tissues.

A **system** is a group of organs working together for a certain function, e.g. the circulatory system contains the heart and blood vessels.

Cells become tissues and organs by cell division. When a cell divides, its nucleus first divides in two, then the cell divides to form two daughter cells. This process repeats, as shown in the diagram.

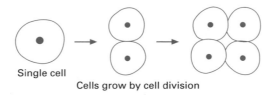

Single cell

Cells grow by cell division

Plant and animal cells

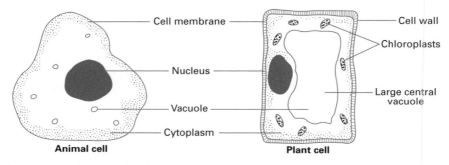

Animal cell

Plant cell

Both plant and animal cells have:

- **Nucleus:** This is the control centre of the cell. It controls cell activities like growth.
- **Cell membrane:** This is a protective layer.
- **Vacuoles:** Plant cells have large vacuoles that contain cell sap (a solution of sugar and water). Vacuoles in animal cells are small or may be absent.

Differences between Plant Cells and Animal Cells

Animal cells	Plant cells
Cell membrane, but no cell wall	Cell wall present
Small vacuoles	Large vacuoles
No chloroplasts	Chloroplasts present which contain chlorophyll to make food

Mandatory experiment: Examine plant and animal cells, e.g. onion cell.

1. Place a small piece of onion skin on a clean glass slide.
2. Add a few drops of water and place a cover slip on the sample.
3. Add a drop of iodine stain to one side of the cover slip and draw it through the sample with blotting paper or tissue paper. The iodine stains the nuclei an orange/yellow colour.
4. Examine under low and then high power with a microscope.
5. Draw a diagram of the onion cells.

Result: The nucleus, cell wall and cytoplasm can be seen.

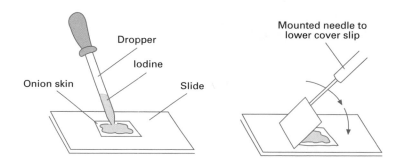

The Microscope

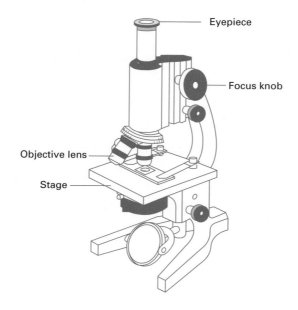

A microscope has five main parts:

- The eyepiece is where you look through.
- The stage is where you place the slide.
- The objective lens magnifies the sample. There is a different lens for low, medium and high power.
- The focus knob allows the stage to be moved to focus on the object.
- The light source can be natural light reflected by a mirror or an electric light bulb.

Chapter **27**
Food and the Stages in Nutrition

Food is needed by living things for energy, growth, repair and protection against disease.

Balanced Diet and Types of Food

A **balanced diet** consists of the correct amounts of carbohydrates, proteins, fats, minerals and vitamins for healthy living.

Food type	Source	Function
Carbohydrates		
Sugar	Jam, honey	Energy
Starch	Bread, pasta	Energy
Fibre	Bran, vegetables	Prevents constipation
Fats	Butter, cheese	Energy
Proteins	Lean meat, fish	Growth and repair
Vitamins		
Vitamin C	Oranges, lemons	Healthy skin and gums
Vitamin D	Milk, cheese	Strong bones
Minerals		
Calcium	Milk, cheese	Strong bones and teeth
Iron	Liver, cabbage	To make red blood cells

Living things also need water to dissolve the food materials and to make solutions for chemical reactions to occur, e.g. respiration, where the food is broken down into energy.

Food and Energy

Food provides us with the **chemical energy** we need to perform our daily functions. Food packets usually give information about the types of food in a packet and their energy values.

Example: Nutrition information per 100 g white bread.

Energy	950 kJ
Protein	8.0 g
Fat	1.9 g
Carbohydrate	48.6 g
Dietary fibre	1.8 g
Total salt	1.6 g

The information on the packet above tells us that white bread contains 950 kilojoules (kJ) of energy for every 100 g consumed. The main food type present is carbohydrate, which provides energy.

It is important to note that fats contain twice as much energy as carbohydrates. A balanced diet should provide us with enough energy for the various activities we perform that day. If too much energy is taken in, e.g. eating too much fat, problems with overweight can result.

Food Pyramid

The **food pyramid** shows the amounts of each common food type that should be eaten by an average adult or child for a healthy, balanced diet.

Level	Quantity to eat
Top (fats, sweets)	Smallest amount
Second (fish, chicken)	Small amount
Third (butter, cheese)	Medium amount
Fourth (fruit, vegetables)	Large amount
Bottom (bread, cereals)	Largest amount

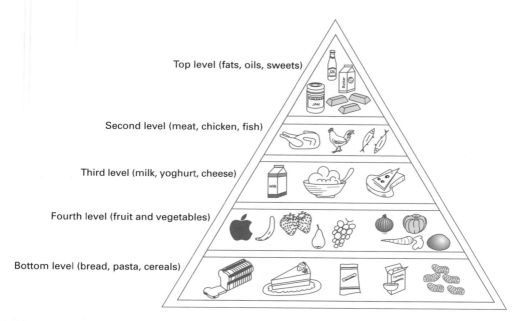

Top level (fats, oils, sweets)

Second level (meat, chicken, fish)

Third level (milk, yoghurt, cheese)

Fourth level (fruit and vegetables)

Bottom level (bread, pasta, cereals)

The amount of energy and therefore food required by each person depends on age, sex (males need more than females) and energy output.

Mandatory experiments: Food tests.

(A) Test for starch

1. Place some starch solution (or food solution with starch in it) into a test tube.
2. Add a few drops of iodine solution.

Result: The solution turns blue-black, confirming starch is present.

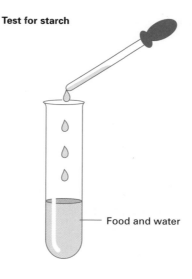

Test for starch

Food and water

(B) Test for a reducing sugar, e.g. glucose

1. Place a solution of glucose in a test tube.
2. Add Benedict's solution, which has a blue colour.
3. Heat the solution.

Result: The solution turns red, confirming sugar is present.

Test for glucose

Heated food and water

(C) Test for proteins: Biuret test

1. Place a solution containing protein, e.g. milk, in a test tube.
2. Add some Biuret reagent, which is a mixture of sodium hydroxide and copper sulphate.

Result: A violet colour is produced, confirming protein is present.

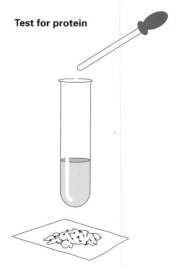

Test for protein

(D) Test for fats

1. Rub a fatty food, e.g. butter, on a piece of brown paper.
2. Allow the paper to dry.

Result: A translucent spot (light can get through) is present on the paper, indicating the presence of fat.

Test for fat

Mandatory experiment: Show that chemical energy in food can be changed to heat energy.

1. Set up the apparatus as shown in the diagram.

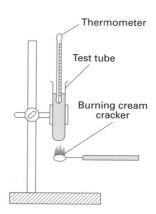

2. Take the temperature of the water in the test tube using the thermometer.
3. Light a piece of cream cracker on a needle and hold it under the test tube, as shown in the diagram.

Result and conclusion: The temperature of the water is seen to rise, proving that the chemical energy in the food was changed to heat energy.

Stages in Animal Nutrition

1. **Ingestion:** The taking in of food to the mouth.
2. **Digestion:** The breakdown of food into smaller soluble particles. There is physical digestion by the teeth and chemical digestion by enzymes.
3. **Absorption:** The passage of the soluble food molecules into the blood from the small intestine.
4. **Assimilation:** This is where the soluble food particles are used by the body cells to make energy and provide cell parts for growth.
5. **Egestion:** The removal of waste food from the body.

Physical Digestion of Food

Physical digestion of food is carried out by the teeth, whereby the food is broken up into smaller pieces. An adult has thirty-two teeth – sixteen in the upper jaw and sixteen in the lower jaw.

There are four types of teeth:

1. **Incisors:** Sharp teeth at the front for cutting food.
2. **Canines:** Pointed teeth for tearing food, e.g. meat.
3. **Premolars:** Flat back teeth for grinding and chewing food.
4. **Molars:** Large, flat back teeth for grinding and chewing.

Structure of Teeth

All teeth have the same basic structure, with the following parts:

- **Enamel:** Hard, non-living material that protects the inside of the tooth.
- **Dentine:** Bone-like substance that is not as hard as the enamel, but which also protects the tooth.
- **Pulp cavity:** This region contains living cells. It contains blood cells that supply the tooth with food and oxygen, and contains nerve cells as well.
- **Cement:** Holds the tooth firmly into the gum.

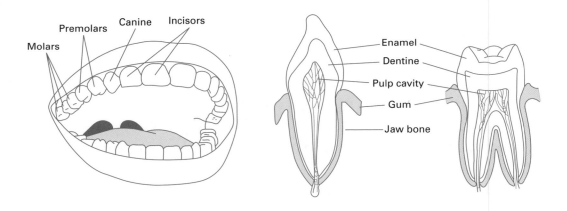

Care of the Teeth

Tooth decay is caused by bacteria. Plaque is a build-up of sugar and bacteria on the teeth. Prevention of tooth decay is achieved by brushing teeth regularly and avoiding sugary foods.

Differences between arteries and veins:

Arteries	Veins
Carry blood away from the heart	Carry blood to the heart
Have thick muscular walls with no valves	Have thin muscular walls with no valves
Carry blood at high pressure	Carry blood at low pressure

Note that valves are necessary in veins to prevent the backflow of blood, as the blood travels slowly (under low pressure).
A section through a vein would look like the diagram.
Capillaries are blood vessels that have very thin walls and connect arteries to veins.

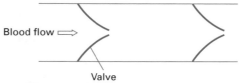

Blood flow ⇨

Valve

Food and oxygen exit through the thin walls of capillaries to the body cells.
Waste materials from the cells pass into the capillaries.

The Heart

The **heart** acts as a muscular pump. Its main function is to pump the blood around the body, delivering oxygen to the cells. The heart is divided into four chambers: the left atrium and right atrium and the left and right ventricles.

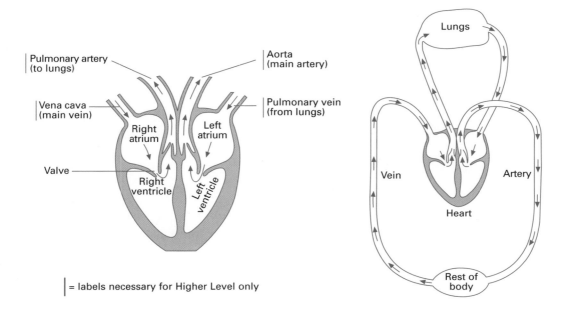

Pulmonary artery (to lungs)

Aorta (main artery)

Vena cava (main vein)

Pulmonary vein (from lungs)

Right atrium

Left atrium

Valve

Right ventricle

Left ventricle

Lungs

Vein

Artery

Heart

Rest of body

| = labels necessary for Higher Level only

143

Flow of Blood Through the Heart

1. Oxygenated blood (blood with oxygen) from the lungs flows in the pulmonary vein into the left atrium of the heart.
2. The blood travels through a valve into the left ventricle. The left ventricle is the main pump of the heart and pumps the blood out through the aorta to the body. The aorta is the main artery of the body.
3. Deoxygenated blood (blood without oxygen) arrives back at the right atrium of the heart through the vena cava. The vena cava is the main vein in the body. It then flows into the right ventricle and the blood is pumped back to the lungs through the pulmonary artery.

Note that the wall of the left ventricle is thicker than the right, as the left ventricle has to pump blood to the whole body, whereas the right ventricle only has to pump blood to the lungs.

Cardiac and Skeletal Muscle

The muscle of the heart is called **cardiac muscle**. Unlike ordinary skeletal muscle, it functions automatically, i.e. it is involuntary (not under our conscious control). In addition, cardiac muscle does not fatigue (get tired), but the **skeletal muscle** of our legs and arms does fatigue.

To prevent heart disease:

*   Take regular exercise.
*   Do not smoke.
*   Keep a balanced diet without too much fat.

Experiment: Show the effect of exercise on (a) pulse rate (b) breathing rate.

(A) Pulse rate

1. A pulse can be felt at the wrist.
2. Using a stopwatch, record the pulse rate for one minute at rest. The average pulse rate for an adult human is seventy beats per minute.
3. Now run on the spot for one minute.
4. Record your pulse rate again for the first minute after exercise. You will notice that the pulse rate has increased.

Conclusion: Exercise increases pulse rate.

(B) Breathing rate

1. Count the number of breaths you take per minute while sitting at rest.
2. Repeat this for a further minute and get your average breathing rate per minute while at rest.
3. Run on the spot for two minutes.
4. Count the number of breaths you take in for each minute for the five minutes after exercise.

Results and conclusion: The breathing rate increases after exercise. As time passes without any further exercise, the breathing rate gradually decreases back to the resting rate.

Chapter **29**
Respiration and Breathing

Respiration

Respiration is the release of energy from food. Respiration occurs in plants and animals.

The word equation for respiration is:

glucose + oxygen = energy + carbon dioxide + water

The type of respiration that uses oxygen is called aerobic respiration.

Respiration and breathing are not the same. **Breathing** in an animal is the taking in of oxygen for respiration and the release of carbon dioxide produced in respiration. In humans, this gas exchange occurs in the lungs.

Breathing in Other Animals

In other animals, the exchange of oxygen and carbon dioxide (**gaseous exchange**) can occur using different structures. For example, frogs are called amphibians as they use gills for breathing in water and lungs for breathing on dry land.

Insects use holes in their exoskeleton called spiracles for gas exchange with the air.

The Breathing System in Humans

- **Epiglottis:** The flap of skin that prevents food from going down the windpipe.
- **Windpipe (trachea):** Carries air into and out of the lungs.
- **Rings of cartilage:** Keep the windpipe open.

Experiment: Show how smoking affects your lungs.

1. Set up the apparatus as shown.
2. The filter pump draws air containing cigarette smoke through the glass wool.

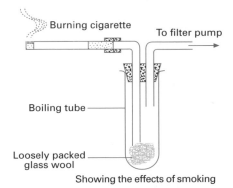

Showing the effects of smoking

Result: The glass wool blackens with the tar from the cigarette smoke.

Differences between Inspired and Expired Air

Air breathed in (inspired air)	Air breathed out (expired air)
Contains 21% oxygen	Contains less oxygen (16%)
Contains 0.03% carbon dioxide	Contains more carbon dioxide (4%)
Contains 78% nitrogen	Contains 78% nitrogen (same)

Mandatory experiment: Show that inspired air contains less carbon dioxide than expired air.

1. Get two sets of apparatus A and B, each containing lime water, as shown.

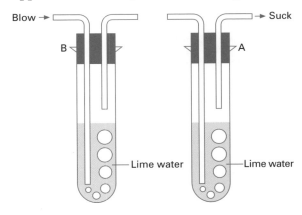

2. Breathe in through A, hold your breath and breathe out through B.
3. Repeat this several times.

Result and conclusion: The lime water in B goes milky first, proving that there is more carbon dioxide in the air we breathe out.

Experiment: Show the products of respiration.

(A) Show that carbon dioxide is produced during respiration

1. Set up two test tubes. Test tube A contains woodlice and lime water and test tube B contains lime water only, as shown in the diagram.
2. Leave for 20 minutes.

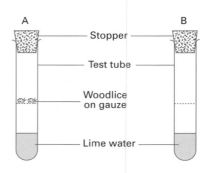

Result and conclusion: The lime water in A turns milky, proving that carbon dioxide is released when the woodlice respire. (Test tube B is used for comparison purposes and is called a control.)

(B) Show that water is released during respiration

1. Set up two test tubes, A and B. Test tube A contains woodlice and a piece of blue cobalt chloride paper. Test tube B contains cobalt chloride paper only.
2. Leave for 20 minutes.

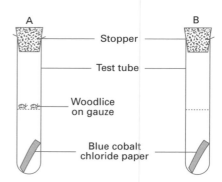

Result and conclusion: The cobalt chloride paper in A turns pink, proving that the woodlice released water vapour. Test tube B is used for comparison purposes.

(C) Show that energy is released during respiration

1. Set up two vacuum flasks, as shown in the diagram. Flask A contains living pea seeds that are germinating, therefore respiration is taking place. Flask B contains boiled pea seeds, which are therefore dead and no respiration present.
2. Leave for one week.

Chapter **31**
Sexual Reproduction in Humans

Sexual reproduction involves **fertilisation**, i.e. the union of a male gamete (sex cell) with a female gamete to form a zygote. In humans, the male gamete is called the sperm and the female gamete is called the egg cell.

The Male Reproductive System

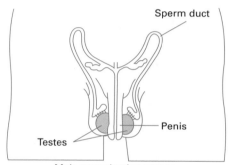

Male reproductive organs

- **Sperm cells** (male gametes) are produced in the testes.
- The **scrotum** is a bag of skin that holds the testes outside the body, as sperm are produced at a temperature lower than the body temperature.
- The **sperm duct** is a tube that carries the sperm from the testes to the urethra in the penis. Along the way, fluid is added to the sperm from glands along the sperm duct, e.g. the prostate gland. The sperm and fluid together are called semen. There is food in the fluid that the sperm can feed on.
- The **penis** releases sperm into the vagina of the female during copulation.

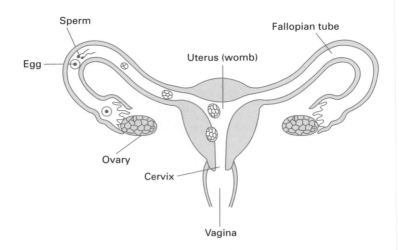

Sperm

Egg

Fallopian tube

Uterus (womb)

Ovary

Cervix

Vagina

The Female Reproductive System

- **Ovary:** Produces the egg cell, or ovum.
- **Uterus:** Where the fertilised egg cell develops into a baby.
- **Fallopian tube:** Where fertilisation occurs.
- **Vagina:** This is the birth canal through which the baby is born.

Puberty

Puberty is the time during which a young person develops the capability for sexual reproduction. It occurs roughly between the ages of ten and fifteen. Puberty in females usually occurs two years earlier than in males.

In the female, sex hormones, e.g. oestrogen, are released, causing body changes such as widening of hips and growth of breasts. The ovaries also start to produce egg cells and the menstrual cycle begins.

Menstrual Cycle

The average **menstrual cycle** lasts twenty-eight days.

- Days 1 to 5: In the first five days or so of the cycle, menstruation occurs. Menstruation is the release of blood and tissue from the inner lining of the uterus if an egg cell is not fertilised.
- Days 6 to 13: A new egg cell is produced in the ovary.

- Day 14: Ovulation occurs, whereby an egg cell is released from the ovary into the fallopian tube.

- Days 14 to 28: A special lining is prepared in the uterus for the arrival of a fertilised egg cell.

If the egg cell is *not* fertilised, the special lining in the uterus is not required and therefore menstruation occurs at the end of that cycle.

If the egg cell *is* fertilised, menstruation does not occur. For fertilisation to occur, copulation must first occur. Copulation (sexual intercourse) is where the erect penis of the male is placed in the vagina of the female and the semen is released. The release of semen into the upper part of the vagina is called **insemination**. The sperm cells swim up into the fallopian tube, where fertilisation takes place. When the sperm unites with the egg cell, a zygote is formed. This zygote divides to form a ball of cells which travels down into the uterus and plants itself in the lining of the uterus. This is called **implantation**.

Note that when fertilisation occurs, menstruation does not occur, as the special lining in the uterus is now required.

The diagram shows fertilisation occurring in the fallopian tube and the fertilised egg cell, which moves into the uterus, where it plants itself.

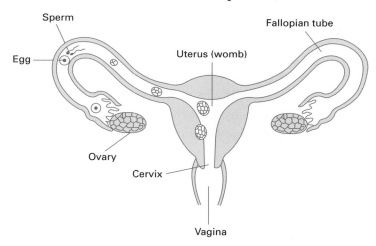

The **fertile period** is the days in the menstrual cycle when a woman is most likely to become pregnant. On average, the fertile period can stretch from day 11 to day 17.

The **gestation period (pregnancy)** is the length of time the baby spends in the womb before birth, usually forty weeks. After implantation, the growing embryo separates from the inner lining of the uterus and is connected to it by the umbilical cord. The inner lining is called the placenta and it supplies the growing baby with food and oxygen through the umbilical cord, as shown in the diagram.

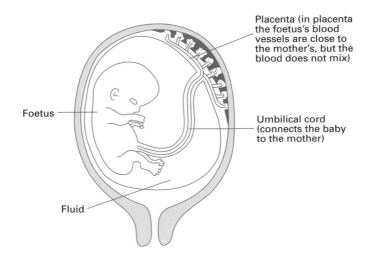

Placenta (in placenta the foetus's blood vessels are close to the mother's, but the blood does not mix)

Foetus

Umbilical cord (connects the baby to the mother)

Fluid

Pregnancy and Birth

During **pregnancy**, the baby is protected from damage by a sac called the amnion, which is filled with amniotic fluid.

By week eight of pregnancy, the arms, legs and all the baby's organs have formed. It is now called a foetus.

Towards the end of pregnancy, the baby's head is usually near the cervix region. When **birth** is about to occur, the muscles of the uterus and the muscles of the vagina start to contract and push the baby slowly out of the vagina. The amnion bursts, releasing its fluid. The baby is born head first. The umbilical cord is cut and tied. The remainder of the umbilical cord and the placenta are released as the afterbirth.

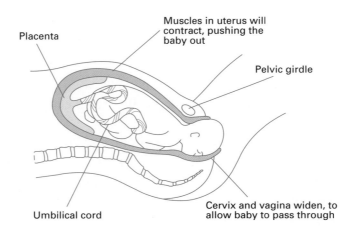

Placenta

Muscles in uterus will contract, pushing the baby out

Pelvic girdle

Umbilical cord

Cervix and vagina widen, to allow baby to pass through

Family Planning

Contraception is the prevention of fertilisation and pregnancy. There are several methods of contraception.

- **Natural methods:** Avoiding sexual intercourse during the time that a woman has her fertile period.
- **Artificial methods:**
  - A condom is a plastic sheath that is worn on the penis to capture the sperm and prevent them from reaching the egg cell.
  - The Pill, which contains chemicals that prevent ovulation.

Chapter **32**
Genetics

Genetics is the study of how features or characteristics are passed on from parents to offspring.

Gregor Mendel, an Austrian monk, is credited with the discovery of genetics. He studied inheritance of features in the pea plant.

Characteristics can be inherited or non-inherited. Inherited characteristics are passed on from parents to offspring. They are controlled by genes. Examples of inherited characteristics are eye colour or the ability to tongue roll (or not) in humans, or the length of stems in pea plants.

Non-inherited features are not passed on from parents to their children. These are developed during one's lifetime, e.g. the ability to drive a car or play football.

Chromosomes and Genes

Genetics is controlled by **genes**. Genes are chemicals made of DNA that pass on information concerning a feature from parent to offspring.

Genes are located on the chromosomes in the nucleus of a cell. **Chromosomes** are threadlike structures in the nucleus of a cell. They are made of protein and DNA and the number of genes they carry depends on the plant or animal. Chromosomes occur in pairs. The following diagram shows a cell with four chromosomes in the nucleus.

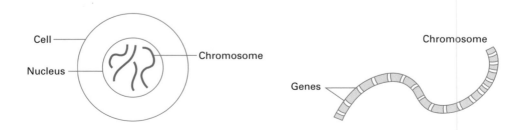

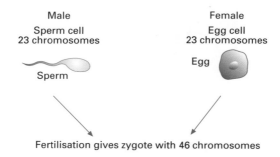

Male
Sperm cell
23 chromosomes

Sperm

Female
Egg cell
23 chromosomes

Egg

Fertilisation gives zygote with 46 chromosomes

Different plants and animals have different numbers of chromosomes. In humans, there are forty-six chromosomes (twenty-three pairs) in all body cells except the sex cells. The sex cells, i.e. the sperm and egg cell, have only twenty-three chromosomes so that if they join together they will produce a cell with forty-six chromosomes.

Therefore, a person has two sets of chromosomes: one set from the mother and one set from the father. Each characteristic is controlled by a pair of genes. Let's examine the gene for eye colour in humans as an example.

The gene for brown eye colour (B) is dominant over the gene for blue eye colour (b). By dominant we mean that if the two genes – the gene for brown eye colour (B) and the gene for blue eye colour (b) – were paired, i.e. Bb, then brown eye colour would result. The only time blue eyes will result is if the two recessive (weaker) genes bb are together.

Genetic Cross

Let's examine a cross between a brown-eyed father and a blue-eyed mother.

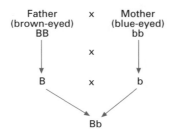

Father   x   Mother
(brown-eyed)   (blue-eyed)
BB   bb

x

B   x   b

Bb

The children are all brown-eyed, as brown eye colour is dominant.

Chapter 33
The Skeleton, Bone and Muscle

Types of Skeleton

- **Endoskeleton:** A skeleton on the inside of the body, e.g. humans.
- **Exoskeleton:** A skeleton on the outside of the body, e.g. crabs.

Functions of the Skeleton

- Supports the body. Without the skeleton, the body would be a big blob of jelly!
- Protects the inner organs, e.g. the skull protects the brain and the rib cage protects the heart and lungs.
- Movement: The skeleton, working with the muscles, enables us to move.

Bone

Bone is composed of a living, or organic, part that is made of protein and a non-living, or inorganic, part that is made of calcium salts. This is why the intake of the mineral calcium in our diet is so important for the growth of bones.
The main bones in the human skeleton are shown in the diagram. The femur, or thigh bone, is the largest single bone in the human skeleton. (Note: H = names of bones required for Higher Level only.)

The Spine (Backbone)

Animals with a backbone are called **vertebrates**, e.g. humans. Animals without a backbone are called **invertebrates**, e.g. earthworm.

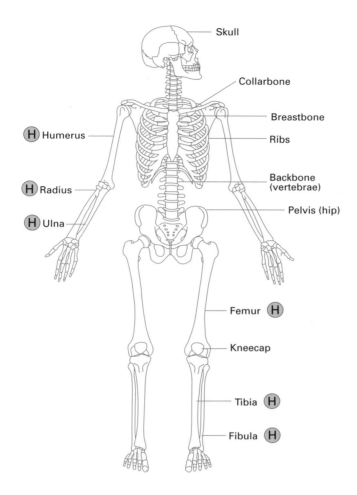

Skull

Collarbone

Breastbone

(H) Humerus

Ribs

(H) Radius

Backbone
(vertebrae)

(H) Ulna

Pelvis (hip)

Femur (H)

Kneecap

Tibia (H)

Fibula (H)

The **spine**, or backbone, in humans consists of thirty-three small bones, or vertebrae, separated by discs of cartilage that allow some movement and act as shock absorbers.

The spine protects the main nerve of the body, called the spinal cord, which runs through the middle of each bone.

Bone Joints

A **bone joint** is where two bones meet.

Types of bone joint:

- **Fused joints:** No movement is allowed, e.g. bones of the skull.
- **Pivot joints:** One bone turns on another, e.g. neck.

- **Ball and socket joints:** Movement in many directions is allowed, e.g. the hip and shoulder.
- **Hinge joints:** Movement in one plane only is allowed, e.g. the elbow and knee.

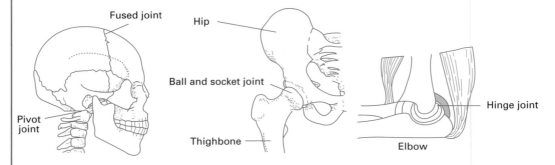

Synovial Joints

Moveable joints such as hinge joints or ball and socket joints contain a fluid called **synovial fluid** and are therefore called **synovial joints**.

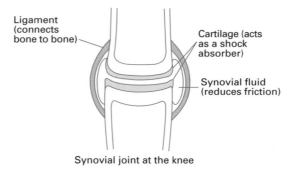

Synovial joint at the knee

Functions of:
- **Ligaments:** Tough fibres that hold bone to bone in a joint.
- **Cartilage:** A soft bone that provides a cushioning effect and prevents the bones wearing off each other.
- **Synovial fluid:** Lubricates the joint and prevents friction and wearing of the bones.

What is the difference between ligaments and tendons?
- Ligaments connect bone to bone. (Remember 'LBB' = 'love bacon butties'!)
- Tendons connect muscle to bone.

Muscles

When a muscle contracts, it pulls on a bone and allows movement. **Tendons** are fibres that attach muscles to bones and allow movement to occur.

Antagonistic muscles are pairs of muscles that pull in opposite directions. A muscle can only contract (get shorter). Another muscle is needed to make them get longer again. A good example is the movement of the lower arm brought about by the biceps and triceps muscles.

Movement of Lower Arm

When the biceps muscle contracts, it pulls on the lower arm, lifting it up. This causes the triceps muscle to relax (see Figure 1).

To lower the arm again, the triceps muscle contracts and the biceps muscle relaxes (see Figure 2).

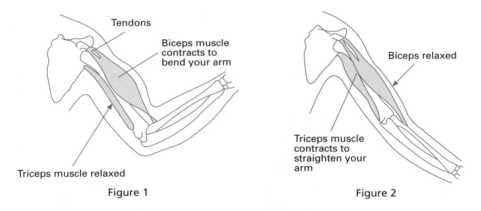

Tendons

Biceps muscle contracts to bend your arm

Triceps muscle relaxed

Figure 1

Biceps relaxed

Triceps muscle contracts to straighten your arm

Figure 2

Thus, the muscles work in opposition to each other and are therefore said to be antagonistic.

Chapter **34**
The Nervous System

Sense Organs

Sense organs react to different types of stimulus in our environment, e.g. the ear responds to sound. There are five senses and therefore five sense organs.

Sense	Sense organ
Sight	Eye
Hearing	Ear
Smell	Nose
Taste	Tongue
Touch	Skin

The nervous system is made up of two main parts: the central and peripheral nervous system.

- The **central nervous system** consists of the brain and spinal cord.
- The **peripheral nervous system** contains nerves that bring messages into and out of the central nervous system.

The nervous system is therefore a system of communication within the body as well as organising the reaction of the body to the information it receives.
A nerve is made up of bundles of nerve cells called neurons. Electrical messages are carried by neurons in a fast, efficient manner. There are two main types of nerves: sensory nerves and motor nerves.
Sensory nerves carry messages from a sense organ to the brain or spinal cord.
Motor nerves carry a message from the brain or spinal cord to a muscle or gland, which carries out a response.

How Does the Nervous System Work?

Let's take an example of a person accidentally touching a hot plate. The skin, our sensory organ of touch, sends a message along a sensory nerve to the spinal cord and the brain, which immediately sends a message along a motor nerve to a muscle in the arm to lift the hand away, as the following diagram shows.

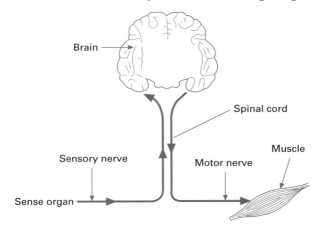

The Eye

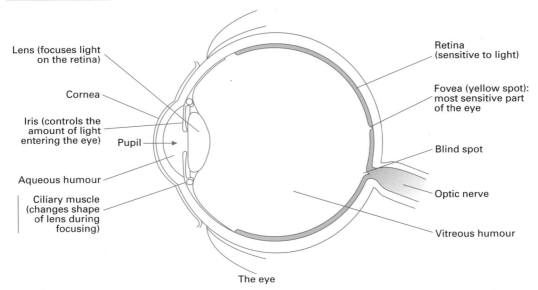

The eye

- **Cornea:** Transparent layer at the front of the eye that allows light in.
- **Sclera:** Outer protective coat of the eye.
- **Pupil:** Hole in the centre of the eye that allows light into the eye.

- **Iris:** Sheet of muscle at the front of the eye that can make the pupil bigger or smaller. It therefore controls the amount of light entering the eye. In bright light, for example, the iris makes the pupil smaller.
- **Retina:** The inner layer of the eye that is sensitive to light.
- **Optic nerve:** Carries light messages from the eye to the brain.
- **Lens:** Focuses the light onto the retina.
- **Ciliary muscle:** Changes the shape of the lens to allow it to see near and distant objects.

Communication between Eye and Brain

When light rays enter the eye, they are focused by the lens onto the retina. The image formed is upside down, as shown in the diagram. This image is sent to the brain by the optic nerve. In the brain, the image is turned the right way up.

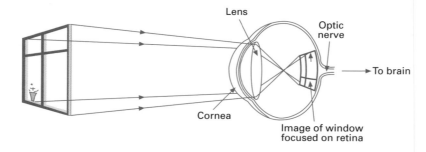

Chapter **35**
Plant Structure and Transport

A flowering plant has the following parts:

- Root.
- Stem.
- Leaf.
- Flower.

Functions of **root:**

- To anchor the plant.
- To take in water and minerals from the soil.
- To store food, e.g. carrot.

Functions of **stem:**

- To transport water and food: xylem vessels carry water up a plant, phloem vessels carry food.
- To support leaves and flowers.
- To store food, e.g. celery.

Functions of **leaf:**

- To produce food in photosynthesis.
- To release water vapour in transpiration.
- To store food, e.g. onion.

Function of **flower:**

- Reproduction.
- Seed and fruit production.

Experiment: Show that the roots absorb water.

1. Set up the apparatus as shown in the diagram. Test tube B is used as a control for comparison.

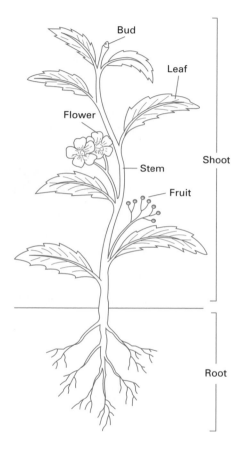

2. Place equal volumes of water in each test tube.
3. Cover each test tube with a layer of oil to prevent evaporation.
4. Mark the level of oil in each tube.
5. Leave for one week.
6. The level of water will have fallen in the tube with the plant but will not have fallen in the other tube.

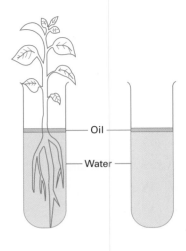

Oil

Water

Conclusion: This proves that water is taken in by the roots.

Experiment: Show the movement of water in plants. In this experiment, the transport of water up a plant by the xylem vessels will be demonstrated.

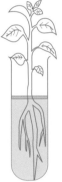

Section showing dots

1. Place a geranium plant in water to which some red dye has been added to colour it.
2. Leave for three to four days in sunlight, then remove the plant.
3. Using a sharp blade, cut sections through the root and stem of the plant.

The dots represent xylem vessels

Result and conclusion: When the sections are examined, red dots will be seen, which indicates the xylem vessels that carry water up the plant.

Transpiration

The loss of water vapour by a plant is called **transpiration**. It occurs mainly in the leaves.

The flow of water through a plant is called the **transpiration stream**. As we have seen, water is taken in by the roots and then travels up the xylem vessels to the leaves, where some of it is used in photosynthesis.

The excess water is released as water vapour through pores in the leaf called **stomata**.

Functions of transpiration:

- To carry water to the leaves for transpiration.
- To cool the plant.
- To carry in minerals from the root.

Factors that affect the rate of transpiration:

- **Sunlight:** During the day, sunlight causes the stomata to open, which increases the rate of transpiration.
- **Wind:** Transpiration is greater on a windy day, as the wind removes the water vapour from the leaf, preventing a build-up and allowing more to escape.
- **Soil water:** The greater the amount of soil water, the greater the transpiration.
- **Humidity:** This is the amount of water vapour in the air. The less water vapour there is in the air (less humid), the greater the rate of transpiration.

Experiment: Demonstrate transpiration.

1. Place a plastic bag around the upper part (stem and leaves) of a plant, as shown in the diagram. The soil must be excluded, as water evaporates from the soil.
2. Make sure that the soil is well watered and the plant is placed in warm sunlight for four to five hours. The plastic bag becomes fogged up with water vapour.
3. Test the drops formed on the bag with blue cobalt chloride paper. They will turn pink. Thus, water has been formed on the inside of the bag due to transpiration from the plant.

Transpiration

Chapter 36
Photosynthesis

Photosynthesis is the process by which green plants make their own food. It is mainly carried out in the leaves of plants. The cells that produce food in a leaf contain chloroplasts, which contain a green chemical called chlorophyll that is necessary for photosynthesis.

Word equation for photosynthesis:

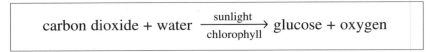

$$\text{carbon dioxide} + \text{water} \xrightarrow[\text{chlorophyll}]{\text{sunlight}} \text{glucose} + \text{oxygen}$$

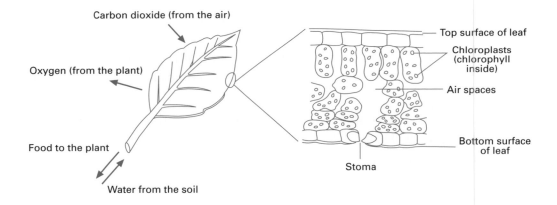

The structure of the leaf is ideally suited to photosynthesis:

- The leaf is broad and thin to absorb maximum sunlight.
- It contains pores called stomata which allow carbon dioxide in for photosynthesis and allow oxygen and water vapour out.
- Special cells with chloroplasts containing chlorophyll make food. The chlorophyll traps the sunlight.
- The water is brought up to the leaf in the xylem vessels, and the phloem vessels transport the glucose to the various parts of the plant where it is needed.

How is the Glucose Used by the Plant?

- Some of the glucose is used in respiration to provide energy for the plant.
- Some is stored as starch.
- Some is used as protein to make cell parts for growth.
- Some is changed to cellulose for new cell walls.

Mandatory experiment: Show that starch is produced in photosynthesis.

1. Place the leaf of a plant, e.g. geranium, in boiling water. This kills and softens the leaf (see Figure 1).
2. Place the leaf in a test tube of alcohol and then place in a beaker of boiling water. This removes the green chlorophyll from the leaves (see Figure 2).

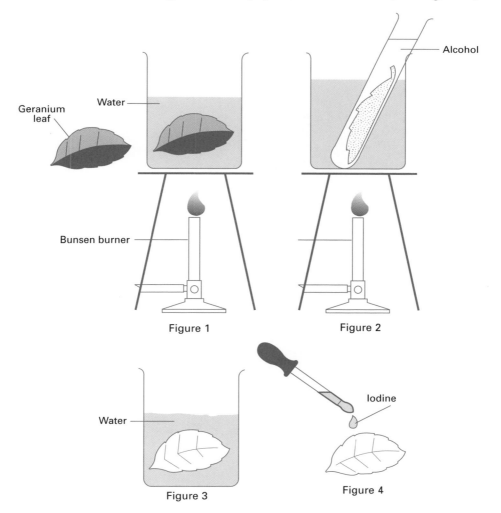

Figure 1

Figure 2

Figure 3

Figure 4

3. The leaf is now white and brittle. Rinse the leaf in boiling water to resoften it (see Figure 3).

4. Spread the leaf on a white tile and add a few drops of iodine (see Figure 4).

Result and conclusion: The leaf turns blue-black, proving that starch is present in the leaf.

Factors Needed for Photosynthesis

- Supply of carbon dioxide, which enters the leaves through the stomata.
- Water, which is transported up to the leaves by the xylem vessels.
- Light, which is absorbed by the chlorophyll.
- Chlorophyll, which absorbs the sunlight.
- A suitable temperature is required for the reaction to occur.

Chapter **37**
Sensitivity in Plants

Plants are less sensitive than animals, but they respond to outside stimuli like light, gravity and water. A **tropism** is a growth response of a plant to a stimulus. **Phototropism** is the growth response of a plant to light. The advantage of this to the plant is that it can get more light for photosynthesis.

Experiment: Show phototropism in plants.

1. Place some cress seeds on moist cotton wool and put them in a box that has light coming in from a lamp through a window on one side.

2. Leave the box in a warm place for one week.

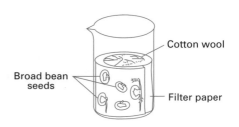

Result and conclusion: The cress seeds will be seen to bend in the direction of the light. Therefore, plants respond to light.

Geotropism is the growth response of a plant to gravity.

Experiment: Show geotropism.

1. Set up the apparatus as shown in the diagram.

2. Place a roll of filter paper into a large beaker, as shown.

3. Fill the middle of the beaker with damp cotton wool.

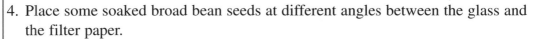

4. Place some soaked broad bean seeds at different angles between the glass and the filter paper.

5. Leave in a warm place for one week.

Result and conclusion: It will be noted that no matter what the angle of the seed is, the plumule (young stem) will grow up and the radicle (young root) will grow down. This proves that roots grow towards gravity (positive geotropism) and stems grow away from gravity (negative geotropism).

Chapter 38
Plant Reproduction

There are two types of plant reproduction: asexual and sexual.

- **Asexual reproduction:** Where only one parent is involved. All the offspring are identical to the parent. Examples: Daffodil bulbs produce new bulbs each year, strawberry runners produce new strawberry plants, mushroom spores produce new mushrooms, etc.

- **Sexual reproduction:** This occurs in the flowering plant, where the male gamete (sex cell) joins with the female gamete (egg cell).

Structure of the Flower, e.g. Tulip or Daffodil

Parts of a flower and their functions:

- **Sepal:** Protects the flower when it is a bud.
- **Petal:** Protects the inner parts of the flower and attracts insects with its colour and scent.
- **Stamen:** Male organ. It consists of a lower stalk and upper anther. The anther produces the pollen cells for reproduction (see diagram).
- **Carpel:** Female organ. It is made up of a stigma, style and ovary (see diagram). The ovary contains the egg cell for reproduction.

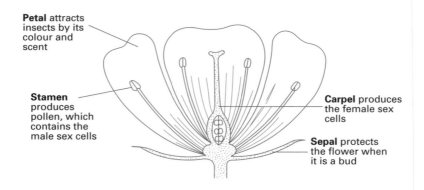

Petal attracts insects by its colour and scent

Stamen produces pollen, which contains the male sex cells

Carpel produces the female sex cells

Sepal protects the flower when it is a bud

Pollination

Pollination is where the pollen is transferred from the anther to the stigma. It can occur by wind or by insect.

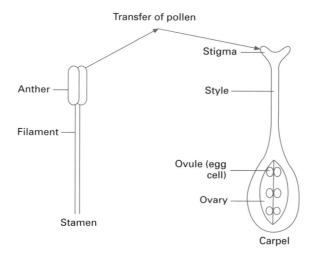

Wind and Insect Pollination

The tulip flower, for example, depends on **insect pollination**, whereas the grass flower depends on **wind pollination**. The structures of the tulip and grass flowers differ hugely, as the following table shows.

Insect-pollinated flower, e.g. tulip	Wind-pollinated flower, e.g. grass
Bright-coloured petals with scent to attract insects	Petals with no scent, as there is no need to attract insects
Small numbers of pollen grains produced	Large numbers of pollen grains produced
Small anthers and stigmas inside flower	Large, feathery stigmas and large anthers hanging outside flower to catch the wind
Nectaries usually present, producing nectar for bees to make honey	Nectaries absent

The structure of the grass flower is very different to the structure of the tulip flower.

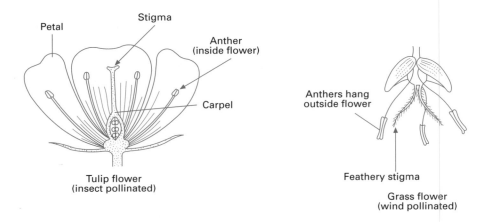

Tulip flower
(insect pollinated)

Feathery stigma

Grass flower
(wind pollinated)

Fertilisation in the Flowering Plant

Fertilisation occurs when the male gamete (sex cell) joins with the female gamete. This occurs after pollination.

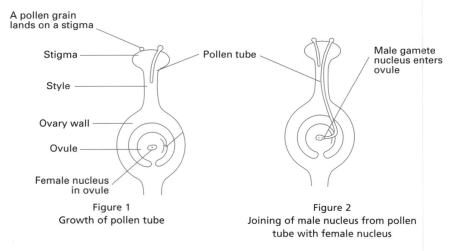

Figure 1
Growth of pollen tube

Figure 2
Joining of male nucleus from pollen
tube with female nucleus

When the pollen grain lands on the stigma of the female carpel, it grows a pollen tube. The pollen tube grows down through the style of the carpel into the ovary, as shown in Figure 1.

The nucleus of the pollen grain, called the male gamete, travels down the pollen tube and joins with the nucleus of the female ovule (egg cell) to form a zygote, as shown in Figure 2. The fertilised ovule (egg cell) becomes the seed.

Seed and Fruit Formation

The fertilised egg cell (ovule) grows to become the seed. The ovary swells to become the fruit. Seeds have a hard outer coat, called the testa, for protection. Inside the seed there is a food supply that is used when the seed starts to grow.

Methods of Seed Dispersal

- **Wind dispersal:** Dandelions and sycamores, for example, depend on wind to scatter their seed.
- **Animal dispersal:** Birds and other animals eat succulent fruits like strawberries and blackberries and egest the seeds later.
- **Water dispersal:** Plants such as the water lily depend on water to scatter their seeds.
- **Self-dispersal:** Pea pods, for example, dry out and burst, scattering their seeds.

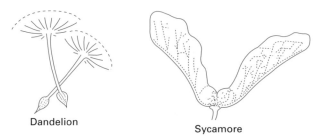

Dandelion

Sycamore

Germination of Seeds

Germination is the growth of a seed into a new plant.
- The hard outer coat (testa) of the seed absorbs water and splits.
- The radicle, or young root, emerges to anchor the seed and absorb water. The food store in the seed provides the energy for the germination.
- The plumule (young shoot = stem and leaves) then emerges. It is hooked to protect the leaves until they go aboveground.
- The stem and leaves go aboveground and the leaves produce food.

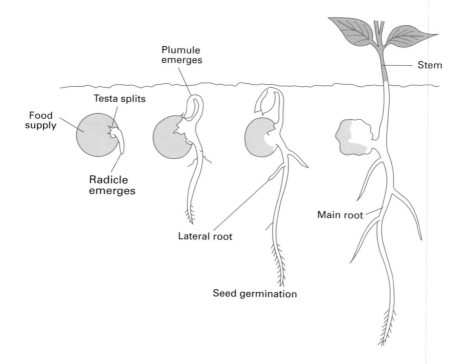

Plumule emerges

Stem

Testa splits

Food supply

Radicle emerges

Lateral root

Main root

Seed germination

Conditions Needed for Germination

There are three conditions needed for germination: water, suitable warm temperature and oxygen.

Mandatory experiment: Investigate the conditions needed for germination of seeds.

1. Set up four test tubes, as shown in the diagram.

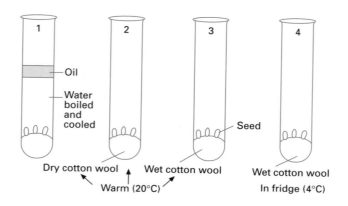

Oil

Water boiled and cooled

Seed

Dry cotton wool

Wet cotton wool

Wet cotton wool

Warm (20°C)

In fridge (4°C)

178

2. Place test tubes 1, 2 and 3 in a warm place (about 20°C). Place test tube 4 in a fridge.

3. Leave the test tubes for one week.

Results and conclusions:

- Seeds in test tube 1 do not germinate, as there is no oxygen. The water has been boiled to remove oxygen and the oil layer prevents any oxygen from returning to the water.

- No germination in test tube 2, as there is no water.

- Germination took place in test tube 3, as the seeds have water, oxygen and a suitable temperature.

- No germination in test tube 4, as the temperature is too cold (4°C).

Chapter **39**
Ecology and Food Chains

Ecology is the study of the relationships between plants and animals (organisms) both with one another and their environment.

A **habitat** is the place where a plant or animal lives, e.g. frogs in a pond habitat.

An **ecosystem** is the habitat plus the plants and animals living in that habitat.

A **food chain** is a feeding relationship between living things in a habitat. For example, in a grassland habitat, the following food chain exists:

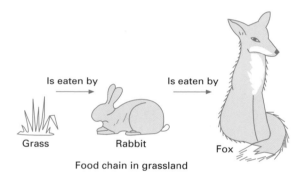

Is eaten by   Is eaten by

Grass   Rabbit   Fox

Food chain in grassland

A **producer** is a green plant that makes food, e.g. grass. All other organisms in the food chain are called **consumers**. The food chain must begin with a producer.

Types of consumer:

- **Herbivore:** A plant-eating animal, e.g. rabbit.
- **Carnivore:** A meat-eating animal, e.g. fox.
- **Omnivore:** An animal that eats plants and animals, e.g. human.
- **Decomposers:** Organisms in a habitat that feed on dead plants and animals, e.g. bacteria, fungi, earthworms and dung beetles. They break the dead material into minerals such as nitrates and phosphates, which plants can use for growth.

A **food web** is a number of food chains linked together. An example from a grassland habitat would be:

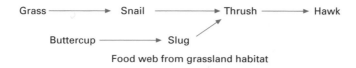

Grass ⟶ Snail ⟶ Thrush ⟶ Hawk

Buttercup ⟶ Slug ⟶ Thrush

Food web from grassland habitat

Feeding Levels and Energy Transfer

The position of an organism in the food chain is called its **feeding level**. Producers, e.g. green plants such as grass, occupy the first feeding level. The second feeding level is occupied by herbivores, e.g. rabbits. The third feeding level is occupied by carnivores, e.g. fox, and so on.

Pyramid of Numbers

A **pyramid of numbers** is a diagram showing the varying numbers of organisms in a food chain. For example, in a grassland habitat, there are far more rabbits than foxes.
Numbers in a food chain decrease as you ascend the pyramid.

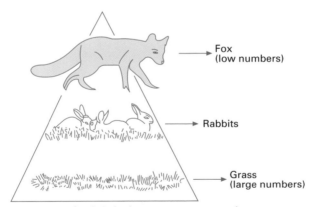

Fox
(low numbers)

Rabbits

Grass
(large numbers)

Numbers in a food chain decrease as you ascend

Energy Transfer in a Food Chain

The primary source of energy in the food chain is the sun. Green plants use the sun's energy to make food in photosynthesis, then the herbivores eat the plants and carnivores eat the herbivores. Therefore, the energy from the sun is passed on from one feeding level to the next.

As one passes from a lower to a higher level in the food chain:

- The energy decreases, as energy is lost when rabbits run about, for example. Therefore, a food chain is usually short, as the energy runs out.
- The number of organisms decreases markedly as it takes a large number of rabbits to provide energy for a fox, for example.

Adaptation

Adaptation is the ability of a plant or animal to change in order to survive in a habitat. For example:

- A rabbit has strong hind legs for running to escape the fox.
- Buttercups have an attractive yellow colour to attract insects for pollination.
- Greenfly use their green colour as camouflage to escape their predators.

Chapter **40**
Ecology: Study a Habitat, e.g. Grassland

There are five main stages in **studying a habitat**, e.g. grassland:
1. Make a simple map of the habitat.
2. Measure and record the environmental factors, e.g. temperature, light intensity, soil water.
3. Collect samples of animals and plants present.
4. Identify and list plants and animals present.
5. Estimate the numbers of each animal and plant type.

The map of the habitat should have a scale giving the dimensions of the habitat in metres. Using a compass, mark the direction of north. There should also be a legend that gives the main features, such as walls, trees, etc., present in the habitat.

Record the temperature of the air with a mercury thermometer and the temperature of the soil with a soil thermometer. Light intensity can be measured with a light meter.

Ways of collecting animals:

- A **pitfall trap** is used to collect small animals that crawl across the surface of soil, e.g. beetles. It consists of a large jar dug into the ground so that the top of the jar is level with the soil. Food bait is usually placed in the jar to attract the animals.

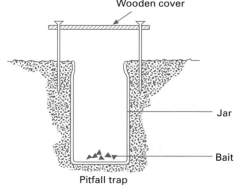

Pitfall trap

- A **pooter** is used to collect small animals, e.g. insects. It consists of a jar with two rubber tubes. If one sucks through one tube, the insect or small animal is drawn into the jar.

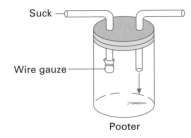

Suck

Wire gauze

Pooter

- A **beating tray** consists of a white sheet that is put on the ground under a bush or tree. The bush or tree is then shaken or hit with a stick. The insects or other small animals that fall from the bush are then collected with a pooter.

Beating tray

- A **sweep net** is used through long grass or hedges to collect insects, e.g. butterflies.

Plant samples are taken in plastic bags and the plants are identified and then clearly labelled.

Further Study of Habitat: To Identify Animals and Plants

Animal Groups

The animal kingdom is divided into two main groups: invertebrates and vertebrates.
- **Invertebrates** are animals with no backbone, e.g. earthworms, insects, spiders, snails, beetles.

- **Vertebrates** are animals that have a backbone, e.g. fish, amphibians, reptiles, birds and mammals.
  - Fish have gills for breathing and scales on their skin, e.g. trout, salmon.
  - Amphibians are animals that can live in water or on land, e.g. frogs.
  - Reptiles have dry, scaly skin and lay eggs on land, e.g. snakes, lizards.
  - Birds have feathers and beaks with no teeth, e.g. robin, thrush.
  - Mammals are animals whose mothers suckle their young with milk and who have body hair, e.g. humans, bats, whales, cats.

Plant Groups

Unlike animals, plants cannot move around and are capable of making their own food in photosynthesis. Plants are identified by the shapes of their leaves and flowers.

Using a Key to Identify Plants and Animals

A key is a simple plan to help you identify animals or plants. The most common and simplest type of key is the dichotomous key, where in each step of the key you are given two choices.

Simple Animal Key to Identify Invertebrates

1.	Legs present . . . . Go to 2
	Legs absent . . . . Go to 3
2.	Three pairs of legs present . . . . Go to 4
	Four pairs of legs present . . . . Spider
	More than four pairs of legs present . . . . Go to 5
3.	Shell present . . . . Snail
	Shell absent . . . . Earthworm
4.	Wings present and visible . . . . Housefly
	Wings absent or hidden . . . . Beetle
5.	Body has less than fifteen segments . . . . Woodlouse
	Body has more than fifteen segments . . . . Go to 6
6.	There is one pair of legs in each segment . . . . Centipede
	There are two pairs of legs in each segment . . . . Millipede

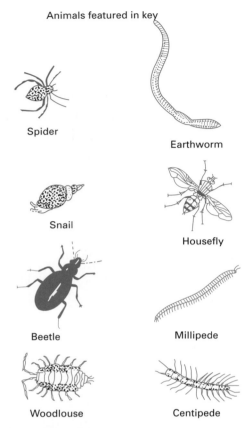

Animals featured in key

Spider

Earthworm

Snail

Housefly

Beetle

Millipede

Woodlouse

Centipede

Simple Key to Identify Plants

The following key can be used to identify trees that lose their leaves in winter.
These trees are called deciduous tees and the key below sets out to distinguish

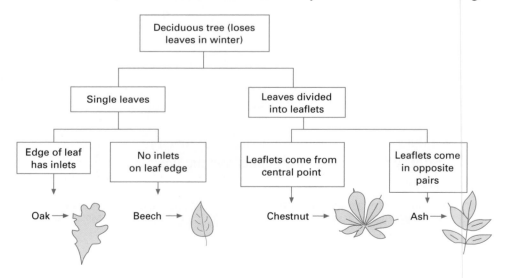

four types of tree, namely the oak, beech, chestnut and ash. The key is set out in a different manner to the animal key above and is called a spider key, as its shape is similar to a spider's legs.

Mandatory experiment: Investigate the variety of living things in a habitat, e.g. grassland, by direct observation.

The class group visited a grassland habitat, which was a field adjacent to the school.

(A) Study the animals in the grassland and distinguish vertebrates from non-vertebrates

1. Using pooters, pitfall traps, beating trays and nets, we were able to observe a variety of different animals living in the habitat.
2. Using simple animal keys like the one outlined previously, we were able to classify the different types of vertebrates and non-vertebrates.

(B) Study the plants

1. Collect a leaf from each plant type in the habitat using plastic bags.
2. Identify the various plant from the leaves using simple keys, like the one described previously, and reference books.

The results are presented in the table shown.

Plants	Vertebrate animals	Invertebrate animals
Grass	Robin	Butterfly
Daisy	Rabbit	Earthworm
Nettle	Thrush	Spider
Beech	Crow	Housefly
Fern	Mouse	Woodlouse

Experiment: Use a quadrat to estimate the number of plants present in a habitat.

A **quadrat** (see diagram) is a square frame made of metal or timber which is thrown at random in a habitat and the types of plant inside it are noted.

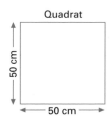
Quadrat
50 cm
50 cm

1. Throw the quadrat at random into the habitat. The names of the plants in it are recorded on a chart, as shown below.

2. The quadrat should be thrown at least ten times at random into various parts of the habitat. Again, note the types of plant each time on the chart.

Results and graph:

Plant	Quadrat number										Total	%
	1	2	3	4	5	6	7	8	9	10		
Grass	✓	✓	✓	✓	✓	✓	✓	✓	✓	✓	10	100
Clover	✓	✗	✓	✓	✓	✗	✓	✓	✓	✓	8	80
Daisy	✓	✓	✗	✗	✗	✗	✓	✓	✓	✗	5	50
Buttercup	✓	✗	✗	✓	✗	✗	✓	✗	✓	✗	4	40
Nettle	✗	✓	✗	✗	✗	✓	✗	✗	✗	✓	3	30

The percentage frequency of each plant can be worked out, as shown in the table.

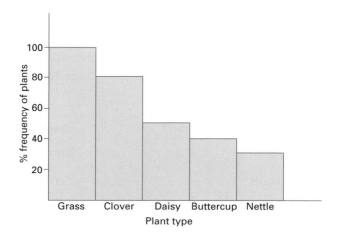

Line Transect

A **line transect** is a piece of string marked at regular intervals that shows changes in the types of plant as one goes across a habitat. The string is usually marked with black tape and staked at each end. The name and height of each plant touching the string at the intervals are noted.

For example, a line transect would show the change in the types of plant as one came from the shade of a tree out into the light.

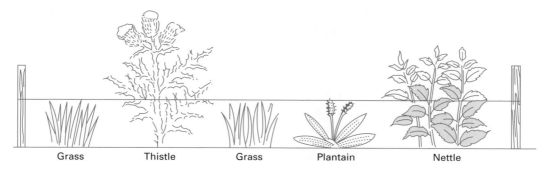

| Grass | Thistle | Grass | Plantain | Nettle |

In the shade, plants like mosses and ferns which need less light would be found. However, as one comes out into the light, sun-loving plants like buttercups and tall grasses would be found.

Competition

Competition is the struggle between organisms for resources such as light, food and water in a habitat that are in short supply. For example, in plants, grass plants have short roots to absorb water from the surface of the soil so as not to compete with plants such as the dandelion plant, which has a large tap root.

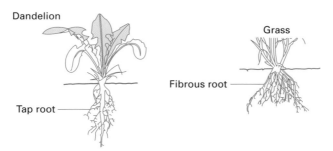

Competition between grass and dandelion for water.
In animals, robins and blackbirds compete with each other for food.

Interdependence of Plants and Animals

Interdependence means that plants and animals depend on each other for survival in a habitat. Some of the ways plants and animals interdepend in a habitat, e.g. grassland, are shown in the following table.

Animals depend on plants	Plants depend on animals
Food, e.g. rabbits depend on grass	Pollination, e.g. buttercup depends on bees
Shelter, e.g. robin's nest in a tree	Seed dispersal, e.g. blackberries depend on birds
Oxygen released in photosynthesis	Carbon dioxide released in respiration

Chapter **41**
Conservation and Pollution

Conservation is the protection, preservation and careful use of our natural resources, including land, trees, rivers and lakes and the plants and animals that inhabit them.

Humans don't have a good record with regard to conservation. We have destroyed habitats in many ways:

- **Deforestation:** The destruction of the world's rainforest, which destroys the habitats of many animals and plants. It also causes **desertification**, i.e. creating large areas of dry, dusty, infertile soil.

- **Poaching and overhunting**, for example, fish, leading to drastic reductions in fish stocks. Due to a lack of conservation, some species can become extinct. In Ireland, bird species like the cuckoo and corncrake are struggling to survive. To try to combat this trend, the government set up conservation projects, e.g. bog lands are now being preserved in many parts of the country.

- **Pollution** means unwanted wastes added to the environment by humans, causing damage to it. Pollution also upsets the balance of nature.

Balance of Nature

The feeding relationships in a habitat such as grassland are finely balanced. Too many or too few of one species can affect the number of another species. For example, if the number of foxes in a grassland habitat was dramatically reduced, this would lead to a huge increase in the number of rabbits, which in turn would severely reduce the number of plants, e.g. grass, in the habitat. Thus, the balance of nature in the habitat would be greatly upset.

Pollution can also upset the balance of nature since it can kill plants and animals in a habitat and therefore upsets food chains in the habitat.

Types of Pollution

- **Air pollution** is the release of sulphur dioxide, smoke and carbon dioxide into the atmosphere by burning fossil fuels. Sulphur dioxide causes acid rain, which damages plants. The release of smoke and dust can cause lung disease and the release of carbon dioxide into the atmosphere causes global warming.
- **Water pollution:**
  - By organic waste such as animal sewage and silage slurry and by excessive use of fertilisers. When these enter our lakes and rivers, they deoxygenate the water, causing fish kills. In addition, the water becomes unsafe to drink as there is disease-causing bacteria in it.
  - Oil spills from tankers destroy the coastline, killing plant and animal sea life.
- **Soil pollution:**
  - Acid rain reduces soil fertility.
  - The use of pesticides: These chemicals get into soil and then into plants. Animals that eat the plants (including humans) are absorbing these poisonous chemicals.

Waste Management

Wastes are materials no longer needed and which must be disposed of, e.g. household waste, building waste, sewage, industrial waste.
Ways of disposing of waste are:

- **Landfill sites**, where the waste is buried in the soil. However, this can lead to water pollution. Landfill sites also produce methane gas, which causes the greenhouse effect and is a greater cause of global warming than carbon dioxide.
- **Dumping at sea**, e.g. nuclear waste. This could cause a build-up of radioactive substances in the sea.
- **Incineration** is where the waste is burned. This releases sulphur dioxide and other toxic gases into the air.
- **Recycling:** Most household waste can be reused, e.g. glass, paper and plastics. This saves on raw materials and their production and reduces pollution.

How Does Human Activity Affect the Environment?

Positive effects of humans	Negative effects of humans
Recycling of plastic, glass, paper, etc.	Illegal dumping
Using wind energy rather than fossil fuels	Burning fossil fuels leads to global warming
Sewage treatment plants	Water pollution by sewage and silage

Chapter 42
Micro-organisms

Micro-organisms are very small organisms that can only be seen by a microscope, e.g. bacteria, fungi and viruses.

Bacteria are single-celled organisms that can reproduce very quickly. Bacteria are found in air, soil and water as well as in our bodies. They can have helpful and harmful effects:

Helpful bacteria	Harmful bacteria
Decay dead plants and animals, i.e. act as decomposers	Cause disease, e.g. food poisoning, pneumonia and tuberculosis (TB)
Used to make food such as cheese, butter and yoghurt	Cause food to spoil, e.g. cause milk to sour
Produce antibiotics	Cause tooth decay

Viruses

Viruses are not cells, but they consist of a strand of DNA surrounded by a protein coat. Viruses cannot reproduce by themselves. They are parasites, i.e. they live inside another living organism. They use the DNA and protein of the host cells to reproduce.

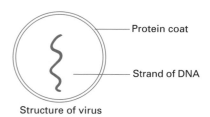

Structure of virus

Diseases caused by viruses include AIDS, colds, flu and polio.

Diseases caused by bacteria include food poisoning, pneumonia and tuberculosis.

Antibiotics

Antibiotics are chemicals produced from bacteria and fungi that are used to cure diseases caused by other bacteria and fungi, e.g. penicillin.
Antibiotics have no effect against viruses. Our white blood cells produce antibodies to attack and kill viruses. Vaccines are also used which, when taken into the body, produce antibodies that can attack the virus if it enters the body.

Fungi

Fungi can be a single cell, e.g. yeast, or consist of long threads, e.g. bread mould. They have no chlorophyll like green plants and therefore cannot make their own food. Some fungi are called saprophytes because they feed on dead matter, e.g. bread mould feeds on bread. Some fungi are parasites and cause disease, e.g. ringworm and potato blight.
There are harmful and helpful fungi:

Helpful fungi	Harmful fungi
Used in baking and brewing, e.g. yeast	Cause food to spoil
Used as food, e.g. mushroom	Cause disease, e.g. ringworm
Used to make antibiotics, e.g. penicillin	Can be poisonous

Biotechnology

Biotechnology is the use of living things to make substances that are useful to humans.

- In industry, bacteria are used to make cheese and the fungus yeast is used in brewing and baking.
- In medicine, fungi are used to make penicillin and bacteria are used to make insulin.

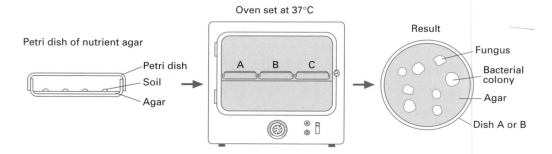

Mandatory experiment: Show the presence of micro-organisms (bacteria and fungi) in the air and soil.

1. Prepare three sterile Petri dishes of nutrient agar. Bacteria and fungi can grow on the agar, as it contains a source of food.

2. Open the lid of one of the plates and expose to the air for fifteen minutes. Replace the lid and seal it. Label this Dish A.

3. Using a sterile spatula or spoon, scatter some fresh soil on the second dish. Again, replace the lid and seal the dish. Label this Dish B.

4. Leave the third Petri dish unopened as a control for comparison. Label this Dish C.

5. Place the three dishes upside down in an oven set at 37°C.

They are placed upside down so that excess moisture does not collect on the surface of the agar. Leave for at least two days.

Results and conclusion: Evidence of bacteria and fungi will be seen on Dishes A and B (exposed to air and soil), but Dish C will be clear. Bacteria appear as shiny dots but fungi appear as fuzzy growths. This proves that there are bacteria in the air and soil.

Appendix 1 Periodic Table

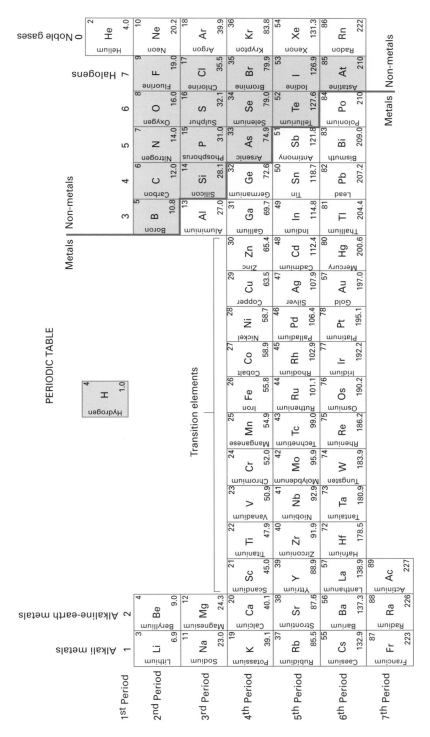

Appendix 2 Laboratory Equipment and Its Uses

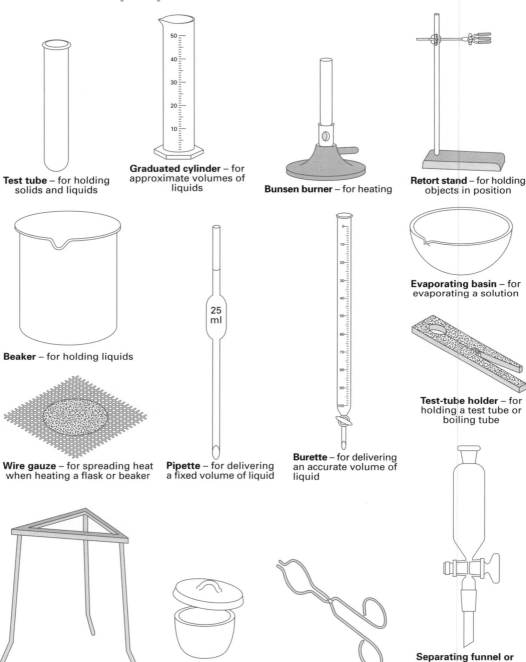

Test tube – for holding solids and liquids

Graduated cylinder – for approximate volumes of liquids

Bunsen burner – for heating

Retort stand – for holding objects in position

Beaker – for holding liquids

25 ml

Evaporating basin – for evaporating a solution

Wire gauze – for spreading heat when heating a flask or beaker

Pipette – for delivering a fixed volume of liquid

Burette – for delivering an accurate volume of liquid

Test-tube holder – for holding a test tube or boiling tube

Tripod – for supporting wire gauze

Crucible – for heating solids to a high temperature

Tongs – for holding hot objects

Separating funnel or dropping funnel – for separating liquids or adding a liquid to a flask

Appendix 3 Hazard Symbols and Their Meaning

The following symbols are put on chemical containers to warn users of their harmful properties.

- **Flammable (or inflammable):** This is a substance that can easily be set alight, e.g. alcohol.
- **Oxidising agents** are dangerous, as they can cause flammable substances to burn more easily, e.g. potassium permanganate.
- **Corrosive substances** attack metal or skin, e.g. strong acids like sulphuric acid.
- **Harmful substances** can cause health problems if inhaled or swallowed.
- **Irritants** are substances that can cause inflammation of the skin following contact.

Glossary

Physics Definitions

acceleration: Change in velocity, measured in m/s/s or m/s^2.

alternating current: Current that changes its direction every fraction of a second. The current supplied by the ESB is alternating, as it is cheaper to distribute. The voltage supplied to households by the ESB is roughly 220 V.

altimeter: An aneroid barometer that measures height (as pressure drops with altitude).

barometer: Used to measure atmospheric pressure. There are two types of barometer: mercury and aneroid. Mercury is more accurate, but aneroid is less cumbersome, as it contains no liquid.

boiling point: The temperature at which a liquid changes to a gas.

centre of gravity: The point where all the weight of a body appears to act.

circuit breakers: They have a bimetallic strip which switches current off when it reaches a certain value.

concave (diverging) lens: Spreads out light rays, e.g. concave lens in spectacles to cure short-sightedness.

conduction: The movement of heat through a substance without the substance moving.

conductors: Allow heat and electricity to flow through them, e.g. copper.

convection: The movement of heat in a liquid or gas. The liquid or gas moves, carrying the heat with it.

convex (converging) lens: Brings light rays together, e.g. lens in a camera.

current: The flow of electrons, measured in amperes (amps) (A).

density $= \dfrac{\text{mass}}{\text{volume}}$, measured in g/cm^3.

diode: An electronic device that will only allow current to flow in one direction.

direct current: Current that flows in one direction only.

dispersion of light: Splitting white light up into its seven colours using a prism.

effects of electricity: (a) Heating effect (b) magnetic effect (c) chemical effect.

electric power = voltage × current, measured in watts (W).

electronics: The careful and exact control of very small electric currents.

energy: The ability to do work, measured in joules.

equilibrium: A body is in equilibrium if it is not moving and is balanced. The wider the base and the lower the centre of gravity, the more stable an object is.

force: Anything that changes the velocity of a body, measured in newtons (N).

friction: A force that prevents easy movement between two bodies in contact. To reduce friction, oil or grease the surfaces.

fuse: Thin piece of wire that heats up and melts when current exceeds a certain value.

heat: A form of energy.

high atmospheric pressure: Indicates dry, sunny weather.

insulators: Do not allow heat or electricity to flow, e.g. plastic.

kilowatt hour: When 1 kilowatt of electricity is used for one hour. This is the unit used by the ESB.

kinetic energy: The energy an object has when it is moving.

latent heat: Heat used to change the state of a substance without changing its temperature, e.g. melting ice to water.

law of conservation of energy: Energy cannot be created or destroyed, but it can be changed from one form to another.

law of the lever: When a lever is balanced, the moments on the left equal the moments on the right.

lever: Any rigid body that is free to turn about a fixed point, called a fulcrum, e.g. crowbar, spanner, wheelbarrow.

light: Light is a form of energy, e.g. a solar-powered calculator. Light travels in straight lines, which gives rise to shadows.

light-dependent resistor (LDR): A resistor whose resistance decreases as light falling on it increases. Used to control street lighting.

light-emitting diode (LED): A diode that gives out light when current flows through it. LEDs are used in displays on calculators, etc.

low atmospheric pressure: Indicates wet, cloudy weather.

magnet: Like poles repel, unlike poles attract. A magnet attracts iron, steel, nickel and cobalt. A magnet points in a north-south direction.

magnetic field: Space around a magnet where it exerts a force.

mass: The amount of matter in a substance, measured in kilograms (kg).

melting point: The temperature at which a solid changes to a liquid.

moment of a force: Force applied × perpendicular distance of force from the fulcrum.

neutral equilibrium: There is no change in the object's centre of gravity upon moving and it stays in neutral equilibrium.

non-renewable energy: Energy that may be used once only, e.g. oil.

normal atmospheric pressure = 76 cm of mercury.

nuclear energy: Energy stored in the nuclei of atoms.

Ohm's law: For a conductor at constant temperature, the resistance is proportional to the current: $\frac{V}{I} = R$. R = resistance, V = voltage, I = current.

opisometer: Measures the length of a curved line.

potential difference (voltage): The difference in electrical pressure between the positive and negative terminals, measured in volts (V).

potential energy: The energy stored waiting to do work, e.g. a wound-up spring.

power: The rate of doing work. Power = $\frac{work}{time}$, measured in watts or joule/second.

pressure: The force per unit area, measured in N/m^2.

radiation: The transfer of heat, in rays, from a hot body without needing a medium to travel through, e.g. heat from the sun. Dark, dull surfaces radiate (release) heat better than bright, shiny surfaces.

reflection of light: Light rays bouncing back off a surface.

refraction of light: Light rays bending when they go from one medium to another.

relationship between mass and weight: Weight = mass × g (acceleration due to gravity), weight = mass × 10 (value of g).

renewable energy: Energy that is replaced, e.g. solar energy.

resistance: The ability a substance has to stop the flow of electrons in a circuit, measured in ohms (Ω).

sound: Sound travels through air at 340 m/s. Light travels faster than sound, e.g. thunder and lightning. The loudness of a sound is measured in decibels. Sound needs a medium (solid, liquid or gas) in which to travel.

spectrum: The spectrum of white light contains the seven colours red, orange, yellow, green, blue, indigo and violet. Remember the phrase 'Richard of York gave battle in vain.'

speed: Distance, measured in metres/second (m/s).

stable equilibrium: A body is in stable equilibrium if it returns to its original position after being tilted.

static electricity: Unlike charges attract each other, like charges repel each other.

sublimation: Heating a substance directly from a solid state into a gaseous state, e.g. iodine sublimes upon heating.

temperature: A measure of how hot or cold a body is, measured in degrees Celsius or Kelvin, where 0°C (Celsius) = 273°k (Kelvin).

thermometer: Instruments that measure temperature. An alcohol thermometer must be coloured and is good for low temperatures. A mercury thermometer is easy to read and is good for high temperatures.

ultrasound: A high-pitched sound that humans cannot hear.

unstable equilibrium: An object is in unstable equilibrium if it does not return to its original position upon being moved.

velocity: Speed in a certain direction, measured in m/s.

volume: Space taken up by a body, measured in cm^3.

weight: The pull of gravity on a body, measured in newtons (N).

work = force × distance, measured in N m. Work can also be measured in joules, like energy.

Chemistry Definitions

acid rain: Rain with a pH of less than 5.5. Gases that cause acid rain are sulphur dioxide and oxides of nitrogen. Acid rain kills fish and corrodes limestone.

activity series of metals: A list of metals placed in order of reactivity, with potassium (K) as the most reactive and gold (Au) as the least reactive.

alkali metal: Group 1 metals, e.g. sodium. These are highly reactive metals.

alkaline earth metals: Group 2 metals, e.g. magnesium. These metals are not as reactive as Group 1 metals.

alloys: Mixtures of metals or a metal and another solid, e.g. steel is mixture of iron and carbon, brass is a mixture of copper and zinc.

atom: An atom is the smallest particle of an element that still retains the properties of that element.

atomic number: The number of protons in the nucleus.

biodegradable: Can be broken down by living organisms. Paper is biodegradable, but plastic is not.

catalyst: A substance that changes the speed of a chemical reaction without being used up itself, e.g. manganese dioxide in the preparation of oxygen.

chemical change: A change in which at least one new substance is formed, e.g. burning paper, rusting iron.

compound: A compound is formed when two or more elements combine chemically, e.g. carbon and oxygen form carbon dioxide.

concentrated solution: A lot of solute in a small volume of solvent.

condensation: Cooling of a gas to a liquid.

corrosion: Where a metal reacts with oxygen to form a compound, e.g. iron reacts with oxygen to form iron oxide (rust). The conditions needed for rusting are water and oxygen. Paint and grease prevent the rusting of iron.

covalent bond: Sharing of electrons between atoms, e.g. chlorine gas molecule.

dilute solution: A little solute in a lot of solvent.

distillation: Separating a mixture by boiling and then cooling. It is used to separate miscible liquids with different boiling points.

electrolysis: The production of a chemical change using an electric current, e.g. water can be split into hydrogen and oxygen by the Hoffman voltameter.

electrons: Are negative and have hardly any mass.

element: The simplest form of matter, e.g. carbon (C).

fossil fuel: Fuel formed from the remains of dead plants and animals, e.g. turf and oil.

fuel: Any substance used to produce heat from a chemical or nuclear reaction.

group: A vertical column of elements in the periodic table. Elements in the same group have similar chemical and physical properties.

halogens: Elements in Group 7, e.g. chlorine. Halogens are highly reactive.

hard water: Does not form a lather easily with soap.

immiscible liquids: Liquids that do not mix, e.g. oil and water.

indicator: Shows by a colour change whether a substance is an acid or a base, e.g. litmus is red in acid, blue in base.

ion: An atom that has lost or gained electrons. A positive ion is formed when an atom loses electrons, e.g. sodium atom loses an electron to become the positive sodium ion (Na^+). A negative ion is formed when an atom gains electrons, e.g. chlorine gains an electron to become the chloride ion (Cl^-).

ionic bond: A bond that is formed when there is a transfer of electrons between atoms. The force of attraction between positive and negative ions holds the bond together, e.g. sodium chloride.

isotopes: Atoms with the same atomic number but different mass numbers.

mass number: The number of protons and neutrons in the nucleus of an atom.

metals: Solid substances that want to lose electrons and form positive ions. Metals are ductile and malleable.

miscible liquids: Liquids that mix, e.g. water and alcohol.

mixtures: Mixtures are formed when two or more substances are combined physically, e.g. salty water.

neutrons: Have no charge and a mass of 1 atomic mass unit.

noble gases: Group 0 elements, which are not reactive as they have full shells of electrons, e.g. helium.

octet rule: Many atoms bond so as to have eight electrons in their outer level.

period: A horizontal row of elements in the periodic table.

periodic table of elements: A table that arranges elements in periods and groups.

pH: A measure of how acidic or basic a solution is. The pH scale measures from 0 to 14. Acids are from 0 to 7 and bases from 7 to 14.

physical change: A change in which no new substance is formed, e.g. melting ice, cutting paper.

plastics: Manmade materials made from crude oil, e.g. polythene.

protons: Have a positive charge and a mass of 1 atomic mass unit.

saturated solution: A solution that contains as much solute as can be dissolved at a given temperature.

solute: The substance which dissolves in the solvent.

solution: The mixture of the solute and solvent.

solvent: The liquid in which the solution is made.

Biology Definitions

absorption: Passing of digested food into the bloodstream in the small intestine.

acid rain: Rain water with a pH of less than 5.5. Acid rain damages the roots of trees and causes fish kills.

adaptation: Ability of a plant or animal to change in order to survive in a habitat, e.g. greenfly use camouflage.

aerobic respiration: Respiration where oxygen is used. the word equation for aerobic respiration is: glucose + oxygen → energy + water + carbon dioxide.

alveoli: Air sacs in the lungs that control gaseous exchange (oxygen in and carbon dioxide out).

antagonistic muscles: Pairs of muscles that work in opposition to each other, e.g. biceps and triceps muscles in the arm.

anther: Produces the pollen, which contains the male gamete. The male organs are called the stamens. The anther is the top part of the stamen.

antibiotics: Chemicals produced from fungi and bacteria that cure diseases caused by fungi and bacteria. Antibiotics have no effect on viruses.

antibodies: Are produced by our white blood cells to protect us against viruses and bacteria.

asexual reproduction: Involves only one parent and there is no union of gametes, e.g. the strawberry plant produces runners which grow into new plants.

assimilation: The body cells use the food for energy, growth and repair.

bacteria: Very small cells. Bacteria can be helpful or harmful. Helpful bacteria make cheese and yoghurt. Harmful bacteria cause disease, e.g. food poisoning, pneumonia and tuberculosis.

balanced diet: Eating the right amount of all the food types, i.e. carbohydrate, protein, fat, vitamins, minerals, water and fibre, for healthy living.

ball and socket joint: Allows movement in many planes, e.g. hip and shoulder.

biotechnology: Using living things to produce useful products for humans. For example, in industry, yeast is used in brewing and baking. In medicine, fungi are used to make penicillin.

bone joint: Connection between two bones.

capillaries: Small blood vessels that connect arteries and veins.

carnivore: Meat-eating animal, e.g. fox.

cell: The basic living unit of a plant or animal.

chromosomes: Thread-like structures found in the nucleus of a cell. All normal human cells have forty-six chromosomes (twenty-three pairs), except the sex cells, which have only twenty-three chromosomes.

ciliary muscle: Changes the shape of the lens in the eye for focusing.

competition: Where animals or plants battle for a resource, e.g. food, in a habitat.

conservation: The protection, preservation and careful use of our natural resources.

consumers: Organisms that feed directly or indirectly on green plants.

contraception: Prevention of fertilisation, e.g. using the contraceptive pill.

decomposers: Organisms that feed on dead plants and animals, e.g. earthworms, bacteria and fungi.

deforestation: The removal of large areas of trees, leading to a build-up of carbon dioxide and less oxygen in the atmosphere.

desertification: The creation of large areas of dry, dusty soil due to deforestation.

digestion: Breaking food down into small soluble particles.

dominant gene: The gene that expresses itself in the offspring when two different genes control a certain feature.

ecology: The study of the relationships between living things and their environment.

egestion: Where the waste food is passed out of the body.

enzymes: Biological catalysts that break down food, e.g. salivary amylase converts starch into the sugar maltose.

excretion: Getting rid of waste materials in the body. The excretory organs are the lungs, kidneys and skin.

feeding (trophic) level: The position an organism has in a food chain. Green plants (producers) are feeding level 1. Primary consumers (herbivores) are feeding level 2. Carnivores are feeding level 3, and so on.

female gamete: Female sex cell produced in the ovary.

fertile period: The time in a female's menstrual cycle when she is most likely to conceive, i.e. day 11 to day 18.

fertilisation (humans): The union of the male gamete (sperm) and the female gamete (egg cell). This occurs in the fallopian tube.

fertilisation (plant): Occurs when the nucleus of the pollen grain joins with the nucleus of the egg cell to form a zygote.

fixed joint: No movement, e.g. bones of the skull.

flower: Produces seeds for reproduction.

flowering plant: Consists of root, stem, leaf and flower.

food chain: The relationship between organisms (plants and animals) based on food.

food pyramid: Shows the amounts of each common food type that should be eaten by an average person for a healthy, balanced diet.

food web: A number of food chains linked together.

fruit: A fertilised ovary becomes the fruit.

fungi: Can exist as cells, e.g. yeast, or long filaments, e.g. mushrooms. They can be harmful or helpful, e.g. mushrooms and yeast.

genes: Units of inheritance, i.e. chemical on chromosomes that controls features.

genetics: The study of inheritance, i.e. how characteristics (features) are passed on from parents to offspring.

geotropism: Growth response of a plant to gravity.

germination: The growth of a seed into a new plant. Conditions needed for germination are water, heat and oxygen.

gestation (pregnancy): The period spent by a baby in the womb, about forty weeks.

greenhouse effect: Certain gases in the air trap heat from the earth in the form of ultraviolet (UV) radiation. The greenhouse gases are carbon dioxide and methane (CH_4).

habitat: Where a plant or animal lives, e.g. a grassland habitat.

heart: Functions as a blood pump. The average heartbeat in an adult human is seventy beats per minute.

herbivore: Plant-eating animal, e.g. rabbit.

hinge joint: Allows up-and-down movement only, e.g. knee and elbow.

hydrotropism: Growth of a plant towards water.

ingestion: Taking in food.

inherited characteristics: Features a person is born with.

interdependence of plants and animals: Plants rely on animals for carbon dioxide and pollination. Animals rely on plants for food, shelter and oxygen.

leaf: Makes and stores food in plants.

lens: Focus the light in the eye.

ligaments: Join bone to bone. Remember 'LBB' – lovely big bone!

line transect: A line made of rope or string which is marked at intervals of 1 metre to show how plant numbers change across a habitat.

male gamete: Male sex cell, called the sperm cell, produced in the testes.

microbiology: The study of micro-organisms, e.g. viruses, fungi, bacteria.

motor neuron: Carries a message out from the brain and spinal cord to a muscle or gland.

non-inherited characteristics: Characteristics a person learns during his or her life, e.g. learning to ride a bike.

optic nerve: Brings light messages from the eye to the brain.

organ: A group of tissues working together to perform a function, e.g. heart organ has skin, nervous and muscle tissues.

ovary: Produces the egg cell, or female gamete. The female organs are called the carpels.

ovulation: Release of the egg cell from the ovary. It occurs on day 14 of the cycle.

ozone layer: Ozone gas protects us from harmful UV (ultraviolet) radiation. Some chemicals, mainly CFCs, present in aerosols damage the ozone layer.

parasites: Feed off a living organism, e.g. viruses.

phloem vessels: Carry food (glucose) from the leaves to the rest of the plant.

photosynthesis: The process by which plants make food.

phototropism: Growth response of a plant to light.

plasma: Transports food.

platelets: Clot the blood.

pollination: The transfer of pollen from the anther to the stigma.

pollution: Adding unwanted waste to the environment, causing damage to it, e.g. air pollution caused by smoke, sulphur dioxide, carbon monoxide from burning fossil fuels.

producer: Green plant that makes its own food, e.g. grass.

pupil: Allows light into the eye.

quadrat: A square frame of wood thrown at random in a habitat to estimate the numbers of plants.

recessive gene: The gene that does not express itself in the child when two different genes control a certain feature.

recycling: Paper, glass, some metals and plastic can be recycled.

red blood cell: Carries oxygen.

respiration: The release of energy from food.

retina: Light-sensitive layer in the eye.

root: Anchors the plant and takes up water.

saprophyte: Feeds on dead organic matter, e.g. mushroom fungus feeds on dead organic matter in the soil.

seed: A fertilised egg cell (ovule) is called a seed.

seed dispersal: Seeds must be scattered to allow them enough space and water, etc. to develop. Methods of seed dispersal are wind, water, animal and self-dispersal.

sensory neuron: Carries a light message into the brain and spinal cord.

sensory organ: An organ that picks up a stimulus from the environment, e.g. the eye.

sexual reproduction (humans): Involves the union of a male and a female gamete.

sexual reproduction (plants): This occurs when a male gamete joins with a female gamete to form a zygote, which becomes the seed of the plant.

stem: Transports water and stores food in plants.

stomata: Pores in the leaf where gases can move in and out.

system: A group of organs working together, e.g. respiratory system.

tendons: Join muscle to bone. Remember 'TMB' – tender mini bone!

tissue: A group of similar cells with a special function, e.g. skin tissue for protection.

transpiration: Release of water vapour from a plant. It occurs mainly in the leaves. The factors that affect transpiration are sunlight, wind, humidity and soil water.

transpiration stream: The flow of water through a plant.

tropism: Growth of a plant towards a certain stimulus.

veins: A blood vessel that carries blood towards the heart.

viruses: Very small organisms that can only multiply inside another living organism. Viruses are not cells – they consist of a chemical surrounded by a protein coat. They cause disease, e.g. AIDS, colds, measles.

waste management: The careful use of incineration, landfill sites and dumping at sea so as not to harm the environment.

white blood cell: Kills bacteria.

xylem vessels: Carry water up a plant from the roots.

EXAM PAPER
WITH SOLUTIONS

Biology

Question 1   (52)

(a)   The diagram shows the structure of an elbow.
      Name **bone A** and identify the **type** of moveable **joint B**.
      Name of bone A *Humerus*   *(3)*
      Type of joint B *Hinge/Synovial*   *(3)*
      N.B. Solidus (1) indicates alternative answer

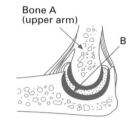
Bone A
(upper arm)
B

(b)   ***Decomposers*** are living things that release useful materials from the waste
      products of plants and animals and from dead plants and animals for reuse
      by living organisms. Name **two** *kinds of decomposers* found in the *soil*.
      Names *Bacteria/Fungi/Worms/Woodlice, etc. (any two)*   *(2 × 3 marks)*

(c)   Water vapour evaporates from cells in the leaves of
      plants and exits the leaves by way of tiny pores in their
      leaves. What is this **process** called? How would you **test**
      the drops of liquid inside the plastic bag covering the
      shoot of the plant shown in the diagram to **show that the**
      drops are water?
      Name of process *Transpiration*   *(3)*
      Test for water *Turns blue cobalt choride pink OR turns*
      white copper sulphate blue   *(3)*

(d)   The diagram is of an
      apparatus used to show that
      exhaled air contains carbon
      dioxide. When performing this
      experiment ***a control is***
      required to show that inhaled
      air contains *less* carbon

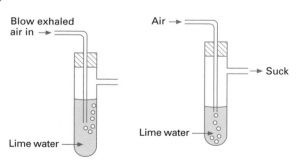
Blow exhaled
air in →
Air →
→ Suck
Lime water →
Lime water →

dioxide than exhaled air. ***Describe, using a labelled diagram, a suitable control procedure.***

(e) The diagram shows the female reproductive system during the ***fertile period*** of the menstrual cycle. What happens in the ovary during this time? What happens to the lining of the uterus during this time?

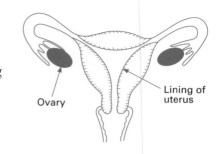

What happens in the ovary?

Ovulation/Release of egg (3)

What happens to the lining of the uterus?

Thickens/Gets rich blood supply (3)

(f) Eye colour, hair texture and many other human characteristics are controlled by ***genes***. Name the ***structures*** in the ***nuclei*** of our cells where ***genes*** are located. Name the ***substance*** that genes are made of.

Name of structures *Chromosomes* (3)

Name of substance *DNA* (3)

(g) Waste management includes: *composting, incineration, landfill* and *recycling*. Pick **one** of the methods of managing waste and say ***how it works*** and give one advantage ***or*** disadvantage of using the method that you have selected.

How it works *e.g. Composting: Plant wastes are allowed to rot* (3)

Advantage/Disadvantage *Advantage: Useful product OR Disadvantage: Slow* (3)

(h) The plant shown in the diagram was left in total darkness overnight and then exposed to strong sunlight for four hours. The ***leaf*** with the foil was removed from the plant and ***tested for starch***. Clearly state the ***result*** you would expect from this test. What conclusion can be drawn?

Result *Covered area does not go blue/black* (6)

Conclusion *Light required for starch production* (4)

$(7 \times 6 + 1 \times 10)$

Question 2 (39)

(a) The diagram shows the structure of a human lung. Air passes in and out of the lungs, via the trachea, bronchi and bronchioles. *Gaseous exchange* takes place in the structures labelled **A**.

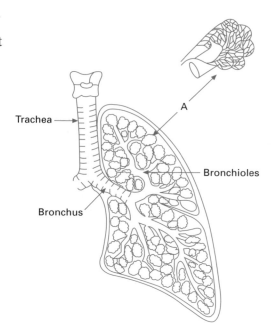

(i) Name *structure* **A**. (3)

Alveolus/Air sac (3)

(ii) How does *gaseous exchange* take place in the structures labelled **A**? (6)

Carbon dioxide enters alveoli from blood (3)
Oxygen leaves alveoli and enters blood (3)

(b) Blood is a liquid tissue. The diagram shows blood viewed through a microscope.

(i) Name **any two** components of blood shown in the diagram. (6)

Component 1 *Red blood cell*
Component 2 *White blood cell*

(ii) Give the *function* of **each** of the components of blood you have named. (6)

Function of 1 *Transports oxygen*
Function of 2 *Kills bacteria*

(iii) The diagram shows the human heart. Why has the left ventricle got a *thicker wall* than the right ventricle? (3)

The left ventricle has to pump blood all around the body (3)

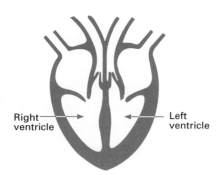

217

(c) The diagram shows a person's *pulse rate* being taken.

   (i) **What** causes a **person's pulse**? (3) *Heartbeat* **(3)**

   (ii) **How** is a person's **pulse rate measured** using this method? (6)

     Counts the beats (3), per minute (3)

   (iii) An athlete's resting pulse rate is 58. After 10 minutes' strenuous exercise their pulse rate was 120. After resting for 5 minutes their pulse rate reduced to 63. **Clearly account for the rise and fall in pulse rate** experienced by the athlete. (6)

     (1) Rise in pulse rate: More oxygen needed or more carbon dioxide to be removed (3)

     (2) Fall in pulse rate: Less oxygen needed or less carbon dioxide to be removed (3)

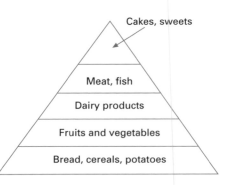

Question 3 (39)

(a) This nutritional information was given on a packet of wheat bran. Wheat bran is used with breakfast cereals and is added to brown bread.

Nutritional Information per 100 g	
Energy	872 kJ / 206 kcal
Protein	15 g
Carbohydrate	26.8 g
(of which sugars)	3.8 g
Fat	2.5 g
(of which saturates)	0.5 g
Fibre	36.5 g
Sodium	0.028 g

   (i) Select **any two nutrients** from the list given and say what **role** each one has in maintaining health. (6)

   Nutrient 1 *Fat*
   Role of 1 *Energy/Insulation* **(3)**
   Nutrient 2 *Protein*
   Role of 2 *Growth/Repair* **(3)**

   (ii) The diagram shows a food pyramid. **Explain how to use a food pyramid to plan a healthy diet.** (6)

     Eat some from each layer/Eat more from bottom/Eat less from top (any two) (2 × 3 marks)

Cakes, sweets

Meat, fish

Dairy products

Fruits and vegetables

Bread, cereals, potatoes

(iii) Tests were carried out on three foods by a pupil in a school laboratory. The results of these tests are given in the table.
A plus (+) sign means a positive result to a test.
A minus (−) sign means a negative result to a test.

Food Tested	Food Tests			
	Starch	Reducing sugar	Protein	Fat
Food A	+	−	−	+
Food B	−	−	+	+
Food C	+	−	+	+

Which **one** of the foods, **A**, **B** or **C**, would most likely be cheese, meat, or fish?   (3)   *B*

Which **one** of the foods, **A**, **B** or **C**, would most likely be crisps or chips?   (3)   *A*

(b) The diagram shows a laboratory microscope.

(i) What are the *functions* of the parts labelled **A** *and* **B**?   (6)

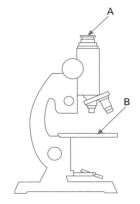

Function of A   *View/Magnify   (3)*
Function of B   *Hold (support) slide   (3)*

(ii) Onion epidermis is a tissue only one cell thick. It is used in school laboratories on microscope slides to investigate plant cell structure using a microscope.
Describe how to *prepare a microscope slide* from a plant tissue.   (6)

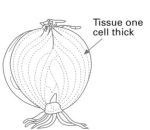

Tissue one cell thick

Put a piece of tissue on slide   (3)
Cover with slip/Add water/Add iodine   (3)

(iii) Draw a *labelled diagram*, in the box provided, of a *plant cell*. (9)
Any three clearly labelled *(3 × 3)*

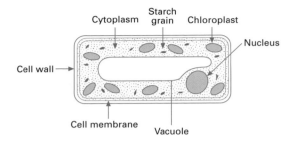

Chemistry

Question 4 (52)

(a) Define the term '*isotope*'. *Same atomic number (3) Different mass number (3) OR Same number of protons (3) Different number of neutrons (3)*

(b) In 1774 Joseph Priestley, an English chemist, discovered oxygen. Name the **two *chemicals*** that you reacted together to ***prepare oxygen*** in the school laboratory. One of the chemicals acted as a ***catalyst***.
Names of chemicals *Hydrogen peroxide (H_2O_2) Manganese dioxide (3)*
Which one of the two chemicals used was the ***catalyst***? *Manganese dioxide (MnO_2) (3)*

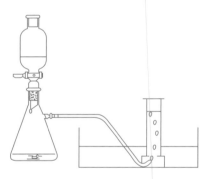

(c) Fossil fuels are burned to provide energy to generate electricity. Give the **name** *or* **formula** of a compound of ***sulphur*** formed when a sulphur-containing fossil fuel ***burns in air***.
Name *or* **formula** *Sulphur dioxide (SO_2) (3)*

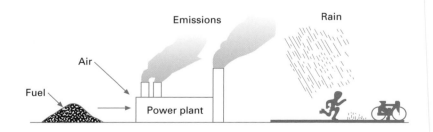

Acid rain is formed when this sulphur compound dissolves in and reacts with water in the atmosphere. Describe the *effect of acid rain* on limestone.
Effect on limestone *Erodes/Damages/Dissolves* (3)

(d) How would you show that *water contains dissolved solids*?
Evaporate (3)
Solid (deposit) (3)

(e) Reactivity tests were carried out on calcium, copper, magnesium and zinc in four test tubes containing an acid. The test carried out using magnesium is shown. State *one thing* you would do *to make the tests fair*. List the **four metals in order of reactivity with the acid**, starting with the *most reactive*. **State one thing** *Same acid/Same size pieces of metal* (3)
Metals in order of reactivity *Calcium, magnesium, zinc, copper* (3)

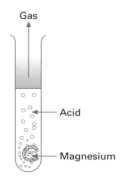
Gas
Acid
Magnesium

(f) Niels Bohr received the Nobel Prize for physics in 1922 for his model of the electronic structure of the atom. Potassium has an atomic number of 19. Give the arrangement of the electrons in an atom of potassium. *2, 8, 8, 1* (6)

(g) Carbon dioxide turns lime water milky. Complete the *chemical equation* for the reaction of carbon dioxide with limewater.

$$Ca(OH)_2 + CO_2 \longrightarrow \text{CaCO}_3 \text{ (3)} + \text{H}_2\text{O} \quad \text{(3)}$$

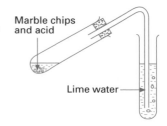
Marble chips and acid
Lime water

(h) The diagram shows the electrolysis of water. Why is *some acid added* to the water?
Why? *So it conducts electricity*
Give a *test* for *gas A*.
Test *Burns with a 'pop'*
The volume of gas **A** is twice that of gas **B**. What does this tell us about the composition of water?
What? *Twice as much hydrogen as oxygen*
$(7 \times 6 + 1 \times 10)$

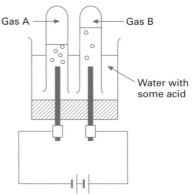
Gas A
Gas B
Water with some acid

221

Question 5

(a) The pieces of laboratory equipment shown, together with some other items, were used to **prepare a sample of sodium chloride**.

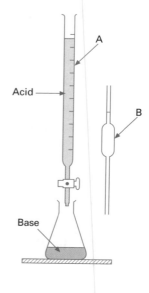

(i) Name item **A** *or* item **B** (3)

  A *Burette* or **B** *Pipette*

(ii) There was 25 cm³ volume of base used in this experiment. Describe how the piece of equipment **A** was used to **measure the volume of acid** required to neutralise this amount of base. (6)

  Read volume before and after release (3)
  Subtract (3)

(iii) Name a **suitable acid** and name a **suitable base** for the preparation of sodium chloride by this method. (6)

  Acid *Hydrochloric acid*   **Base** *Sodium hydroxide*

(iv) Write a **chemical equation** for the reaction between the **acid** and the **base** that you have named. (6)

  $HCl + NaOH$ (3) $\rightarrow$ $NaCl + H_2O$ (3)

(b) Different plastics have different properties. The dust pan and brush set shown is made from **two different plastics**. The bristles are made of **type A** and the other parts are made of **type B** plastic. Give **one property** of **type A** and **one property** of **type B** plastic that that make them suitable for their use in this product. (6)

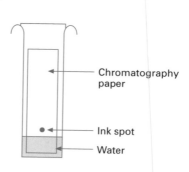

Property of type A *Flexible, tough* (3)
Property of type B *Can be moulded, light* (3)

(c) A spot of water-soluble ink was put on a piece of chromatography paper and set up as shown in the diagram. The ink used was a **mixture** of different coloured dyes.

(i) What happens to the ink spot as the water moves up the paper? (3)

  Different colours appear (3)

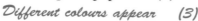

Chromatography paper

Ink spot

Water

(ii) What would happen to a spot of water-soluble ink consisting of a *single coloured dye* if it were used in the above experiment? (3)

Colour remains the same (3)

(d) Study the diagram carefully. It *shows the ways that the particles of gases and solids occupy space*.

The particles of *gas* have *lots of space* and *move randomly* at high speeds in three dimensions and *collide* with each other and with their container. The arrows represent the velocities of the gas particles.

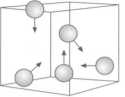

Particles of a gas

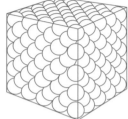

Particles of a solid

The particles of a *solid* are *packed closely together* and *cannot move around* but they can *vibrate*.

Give **one** *property of a gas* and **one** *property of a solid*, that you have observed, and is consistent with (matches) this micro-view of these states of matter. (6)

One property of a gas *No fixed shape, flows* (3)
One property of a solid *Fixed shape, does not flow* (3)

Question 6 (39)

(a) The composition of air can be investigated in different ways.
Two experiments are shown in the diagram.

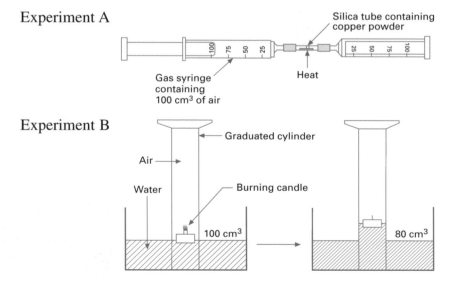

Experiment A

Silica tube containing copper powder

Gas syringe containing 100 cm³ of air

Heat

Experiment B

Graduated cylinder

Air

Water

Burning candle

100 cm³

80 cm³

In **Experiment A** the air was pushed repeatedly over the heated copper powder and only 79 cm³ of gas remained at the end of the experiment.

(i) Why is it necessary to let the apparatus cool down before measuring the volume of the remaining gas? (3)

Volume of gas depends on temperature (3)

(ii) Why did the volume of gas decrease and then remain steady? (3)

Oxygen used (3)

(iii) What is the remaining gas mainly composed of? (3)

Nitrogen (3)

(iv) Experiment **B** is less accurate than Experiment **A**. Give a reason why this is so. (6)

Graduated cylinder not as accurate as gas syringe (6)

(b) (i) Show, clearly using shading and labelling, the *location* of the *alkaline earth metals* on the blank periodic table given. (3)

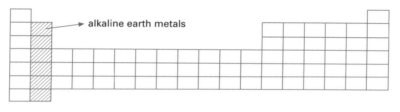

alkaline earth metals

(3)

(ii) Name an *alkaline earth metal*.

Name *Magnesium (3)*

(c) The millennium spire, in Dublin, is made from steel. Iron and steel can suffer from *corrosion*.

Iron and steel show *visible signs of corrosion*.

Give one visible sign of corrosion.

Change of colour/Rust (3)

Oxygen and water together are necessary for the corrosion of iron or steel.

Describe, with the aid of labelled diagrams, experiments to show that:

(i) *oxygen alone* will *not* lead to the *corrosion of iron (or steel)*

(ii) *water alone* will *not* lead to the *corrosion of iron (or steel)*. (15)

Place iron nails in A and B (6)

Remove water from A using a drying agent (calcium chloride) (3)

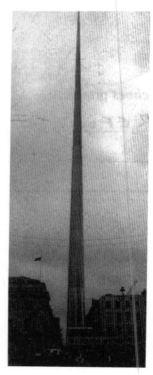

224

Remove oxygen from B using boiled water (3) and oil (3) (6)

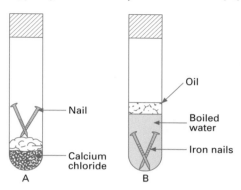

A   B

Physics

Question 7   (52)

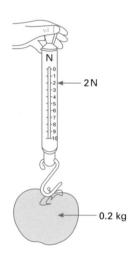

(a) A pupil measured the **weight** of an apple of **mass** 0.2 kg using a spring balance and got a reading of 2 N. Distinguish between **weight** and **mass**.

Weight is a force/pull of gravity   *(3)*

Mass is an amount of matter   *(3)*

Weight = mass × g   *(6)*

(b) How are **echoes** produced?

Reflected/Bounced off   *(3)*

Sound   *(3)*

(c) A girl of mass 60 kg (weight 600 N) climbed a 6 m high stairs in 15 seconds.

Calculate the **work** she did and the average **power** she developed while climbing the stairs.

Work *3600*   *(3)*

Power *240*   *(3)*

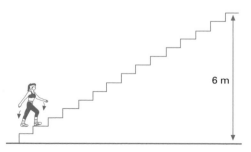

(d) What is *refraction* of light?
Give an everyday example of an effect caused by refraction.
What? *Bending of light*   (3)
Example *Rod in water appears bent*   (3)

(e) Define *temperature* and give a *unit* used to express temperature measurements.

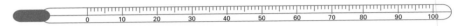

Definition *Degree of hotness or coldness*   (3)
Unit *Degrees Celsius / Kelvin / Fahrenheit*   (3)

(f) Explain, clearly, the *safety role* of *fuses* in household electrical circuits.
Fuse melts or breaks   (3)   *Cuts off currents*   (3)

(g) Name the mode of *heat transfer* from the hot liquid, through the *spoon*, to the hand.
Name *Conduction*   (3)
Heat moves in liquids by convection. Give **one** *difference* between convection and the way heat moves along the spoon.
Difference *In convection liquid OR gas moves carrying heat*   (3)

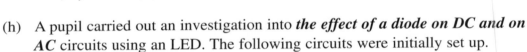

(h) A pupil carried out an investigation into *the effect of a diode on DC and on AC* circuits using an LED. The following circuits were initially set up.

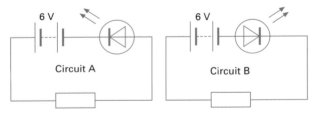

What is *observed* in circuit **A** and in circuit **B**?
Circuit A *LED lights (glows)*   (3)
Circuit B *LED does not light (glow)*   (3)
When the batteries in circuits **A** and **B** were replaced by 6 V AC supplies, the LEDs glowed dimly in both circuits. Explain this *observation*.
Explanation *AC changes direction frequently / Only half current passes through LED*   (4)

$(7 \times 6 + 1 \times 10)$

Question 8   (39)

(a) (i)   Why is the word **Ambulance** painted in reverse on
           the front of many ambulances?   (3)
           Why? *When drivers look in mirrors they see*
           'ambulance'   *(3)*

(ii) A pupil made a ***simple periscope*** using two plane (flat) mirrors. The
      mirrors were arranged as shown in the diagram. The pupil looked
      through the periscope at the word 'Science' written on a card pinned to
      the laboratory wall.

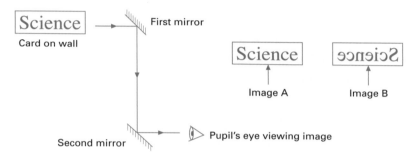

Did the pupil see **image A** *or* **image B** when she looked through the
periscope? Give a ***reason*** for your answer.   (9)
Image? *A*   *(3)*
Reason *Double reflection*   *(6)*

(b) Describe an experiment to show the ***expansion of water*** when it
     freezes. You may include a labelled diagram if you wish.   (9)
     Fill bottle with water and seal   *(3)*
     Place in freezer   *(3)*
     Bottle bursts   *(3)*

(c) The graph is a ***cooling curve***. The substance used in this experiment was
     naphthalene. Naphthalene has a melting point of 80°C.
     The rate of heat loss was constant throughout the experiment.

(i) What is *happening* to the naphthalene between points **A** and **B** on the graph? (3)

Freezes/changes from liquid to solid

(3)

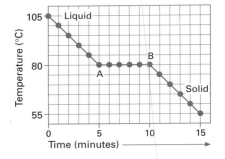

(ii) What is the **heat loss**, between points **A** and **B**, on the curve called? (3)

Latent heat *(3)*

(d) In Ireland **90 per cent of electricity** is generated **by burning fossil fuels** compared to other European countries who have an average of 50 per cent use of fossil fuels and a 30 per cent use of fossil fuels in the USA.

(i) List **two *disadvantages***, excluding acid rain, of this heavy reliance on fossil fuels for the production of electricity. (6)

Disadvantage one *Global warming* *(3)*
Disadvantage two *Rising costs* *(3)*

(ii) Suggest **two *alternative sources*** of energy for the generation of electricity in Ireland. (6)

Source one *Solar/Tidal* *(3)*
Source two *Wind/Hydroelectric* *(3)*

Question 9 (39)

(a) Robert Hooke (1635–1703) made a number of discoveries including the effect of force on elastic bodies now known as Hooke's law. **State Hooke's law.** (6)

Hooke's law *Extension (3) depends directly on force supplied (3)*
A student was given a box of identical springs and asked to analyse them so that they could be used as newton meters. The student performed an experiment, using the apparatus shown in the diagram, on one of the springs.
In the experiment the student measured the increase in length of the spring caused by a number of weights. The spring was tested to destruction (that is, weights were added until the spring was damaged). The data from the experiment is given in the table.

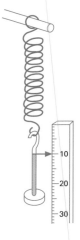

Weight (N)	0.0	0.4	0.8	1.2	1.6	2.0	2.4
Extension (cm)	0.0	2.0	4.0	6.0	8.0	8.5	8.6

(i) Plot a **graph of extension** (increase in length) **against weight** (*x*-axis) in the grid provided on the right.   (9)

(ii) Use the graph to find the **weight** that would produce an **extension** of 5 cm in the spring.   (3)
Weight *1N (± 0·1)*

(iii) Study your graph carefully. The spring obeys Hooke's law for the earlier extensions and then when the spring becomes damaged it does not appear to do so. Estimate, from your graph, **the weight after the addition of which the law seems no longer to apply**.   (3)
1·6–2·0 N

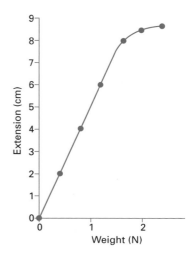

(b) Components, e.g. bulbs, in electrical circuits can be connected in **series** or in **parallel**.

(i) It is noticed that, when one headlight fails (blows) in a car, the second remains lighting.
State **the way the headlights are connected** and give a **reason** why this mode of connection is used.   (6)
State the way *Parallel*   *(3)*
Reason *Safety/If one blows the others stay on*   *(3)*

(ii) All of the bulbs go out in an old set of Christmas tree lights when one of bulbs fails (blows). In **what way are the bulbs connected** in this set of lights? Explain why, when **one bulb blows, they all go out**.   (6)
What way? *Series*   *(3)*
Explain *Circuit is broken*   *(3)*

(iii) Calculate the **resistance of the filament** of a car headlamp when 12 V produces a current of 5 A in it. In what unit is resistance measured?   (6)
Resistance $\dfrac{12}{5} = 2·4$ *(3)*

Unit of resistance *Ohm (Ω)*   *(3)*